AF478547

Powell's   Richard Phillips & Adolf Dietrich (No
39.95/4.98   PC
Art & Graphic Design   100910

RICHARD PHILLIPS
ADOLF DIETRICH

PAINTING
AND
MISAPPROPRIATION

CONTRIBUTIONS BY

RICHARD PHILLIPS

BEATRIX RUF

DOROTHEE MESSMER

PUBLISHED BY SWISS INSTITUTE CONTEMPORARY ART NEW YORK

RICHARD PHILLIPS
ADOLF DIETRICH
PAINTING AND MISAPPROPRIATION

Published in conjunction with the exhibition
organized by Swiss Institute Contemporary Art,
New York and Kunstmuseum Thurgau,
Kartause Ittingen.
Curated by Gianni Jetzer and Richard Phillips.
Curator Adolf Dietrich Estate: Dorothee Messmer

EXHIBITION ITINERARY
Swiss Institute Contemporary Art, New York
May 6–June 26 2010

Kunstmuseum Thurgau, Kartause Ittingen
June–August 2011

CATALOGUE
Published by Swiss Institute, New York
Editor: Gianni Jetzer
Editorial Coordination: Piper Marshall
Authors: Dorothee Messmer,
Richard Phillips, Beatrix Ruf
Translator (THE DIETRICH ENIGMA):
Susan Bernofsky
Editing (IN CONVERSATION): Tova Carlin
Copy editing: Polly Watson
Graphic Design: Li, Inc.
Photographer: Daniel Perez
Printed in Switzerland

INSTITUTIONS

Swiss Institute Contemporary Art
495 Broadway / 3rd Floor
New York, NY 10012
TEL (212) 925-2035
info@swissinstitute.net
www.swissinstitute.net

SI Staff
Director: Gianni Jetzer
Assistant Curator: Piper Marshall
Head of Development: Leonie Kruizenga
Gallery Manager: Clément Delepine
Bookkeeper: Wella Yunitasari
Head of Installation: Mike Levy
Installer: Steve Gunn
Interns: Patrick Bertschy, Kurumi Kido
and Elise Lammer

SI Board
Chair: Fabienne P. Abrecht
Honorary Chair: H.E. Ambassador Christoph Bubb,
Consul General of Switzerland in New York
Secretary: Hans F. Kaeser
Treasurer: Daniel H. Sigg
Trustees: Marcel Biedermann Anne Keller,
Christian Marclay, James McGivney,
Dale E. Miller, Emma Reeves, Catherine Scharf,
Andreas Spillmann

Kunstmuseum Thurgau
Kartause Ittingen
CH-8532 Warth
Tel 052 748 41 20
kunstmuseum@tg.ch
www.kunstmuseum.tg.ch

Director: Markus Landert
Curator: Dorothee Messmer
Back office: Corinne Rüegg
Secretary: Madeleine Baumann

Shop Manager: Käthy Wild
Museum Education: Brigitt Näpflin
Head of Installation: Gianni Kuhn
Installer: Gabriele Mühlebach, Colin Würgler

This catalogue is supported by Lotteriefonds
des Kantons Thurgau and Thurgauische
Kulturstiftung Ottoberg.

SI programming is supported by Pro-Helvetia—
the Swiss Arts Council and by public funds from
the New York City Department of Cultural Affairs.

DISTRIBUTED BY
Worldwide:
D.A.P. Distributed Art Publishers
155 Sixth Avenue, 2nd floor
New York, New York 10013
order@dapinc.com
www.artbook.com

Switzerland:
Markus Wieser
AVA Verlagsauslieferung AG
Centralweg 16, CH-8910 Affoltern a.A.
Tel: +41 44 762 42 00
Fax: +41 44 762 42 10
wieser@bluewin.ch

© 2010 the artists, the authors
Swiss Institute Contemporary Art,
Kunstmuseum Thurgau, Kartause Ittingen

ISBN: 978-1-884692-08-6

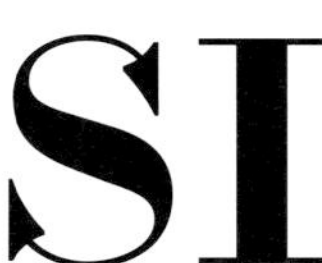

FOREWORD

Kunstmuseum Thurgau and Swiss Institute are pleased to present a unique exhibition catalogue pairing historical paintings by the late Swiss artist Adolf Dietrich with recent paintings by American artist Richard Phillips. The encounter results in a complex, multi-layered dialogue beyond categorizations.

Adolf Dietrich is characterized as one of the leading Swiss painters of the 20th century and bizarrely also as naïve artist. Richard Phillips by contrast is a contemporary painter, who pushes the medium to its limits by choice of provocative themes, a unique painting style as well as by the sheer intensity of his gigantic compositions.

Since 2003, Richard Phillips has repeatedly painted after Dietrich, pushing the boundaries of appropriation to the extreme. Instead of painting after a well-known position from modernism (as Sherri Levine did in the Eighties), Phillips selects a painter, whose fame barely crossed the Swiss borders and who was received highly controversially. Rather than questioning whether any art is truly original, Phillips investigates the discrepancy between appropriation and misappropriation.

The juxtaposition of <u>Painting and Misappropriation</u> is one of distinction and affinity. Dietrich and Phillips share the same subjects: animals, people and landscapes while both enhance figuration stylistically to a degree of artificiality that goes far beyond the depiction of reality.

The pairing of the two oeuvres provokes a radical new reading. Phillips' work gets often criticized for being too literal, while Dietrich's art has been said to be naïve. The cross-pollination of the respective work by the other's misappropriation projects a new light on both. It enhances the classic qualities of Richard Phillips' paintings in their contemporary grandeur and reciprocally makes evident the radical nature of Adolf Dietrich's compositions.

Kunstmuseum Thurgau and Swiss Institute warmly thank the various lenders, who had to do without their favorite works for a long time. We would also like to thank Pro Helvetia, the Swiss Arts Council as well as the Lotteriefonds des Kantons Thurgau, who both generously supported this ambitious project.

But first and foremost we would like to thank Richard Phillips for his ongoing involvement and curiosity in regards of his late colleague's work. The introduction of Adolf Dietrich into 21st century America as part of a contemporary discourse underlines the timelessness of this important modernist Swiss painter.

Gianni Jetzer
Director Swiss Institute New York

Markus Landert
Director Kunstmuseum Thurgau

Misappropriation:
In Defense of the Real Adolf Dietrich

RICHARD PHILLIPS

KRONENHALLE

I was first introduced to Adolf Dietrich's (1877–1957) work in 2003 by the artist Peter Fischli following a dinner at the legendary Kronenhalle restaurant in Zurich. After our meal, I accompanied Peter on a tour of the restaurant's collection where, after seeing works by Matisse, Kandinsky, Braque, and Picasso, I was led into a dining room on the second floor and shown a pencil drawing of two squirrels in a tree. I was told that the drawing was by an early twentieth-century artist considered a "Swiss national treasure." I was surprised by the drawing, struck by the unique qualities of realism carried out by the artist's extraordinary sensitivity to light and tone and by his democratic recording of detail, from the squirrel's fur to the trees' bark to the snow's melting surface. There seemed to be a willingness to invest in the life of the image far beyond any initial painterly representation. The effect of such commitment to rendering drew out the specificity (and thus psychology and attitude) of place and of the animals, which, imbued with such intensity, seemed to take on human quali-

ties. Within the context of works by modern masters, all with their recognizable styles, Dietrich's drawing truly stuck out, seeming all the more masterful.

While Dietrich may have been a "national Swiss treasure," I soon came to the realization that it was a reputation he'd acquired for the wrong reasons. In my mind, he was, and still is, a completely misunderstood artist. Since there are no texts on Dietrich in English, I have been at the mercy of whatever limited information I have been able to find (or have had translated into English), all of which claimed the artist, whose work stylistically shared some of the formal traits of so-called "naïve artists," to be an "outsider artist." Such mislabeling certainly has had a negative effect on the trajectory of Dietrich's career and has severely limited his international exposure to a broader, critically engaged audience.

In 2004, with little more than a rough idea of his output and very little knowledge about the artist's biography (and a great deal of misunderstanding, I later determined), I began work on a large-scale painting after Dietrich's ZWEI EICHHÖRNCHEN (Two Squirrels, 1948). The piece, titled SIMILAR TO SQUIRRELS (2004), was intended for an exhibition at Le Consortium in Dijon themed around represen-

---

RICHARD PHILLIPS is an artist who lives and works in New York.

ADOLF DIETRICH, TOUCAN, 1927, oil on cardboard, 18 x 15" / PFEFFERVOGEL, Öl auf Karton, 46 x 38 cm. (PHOTO: KUNSTMUSEUM THURGAU, ITTINGER MUSEUM, WARTH)

First published in
Parkett no. 87/2010.
Reprint with the kind
permission of
Parkett Publishers,
Zurich / New York

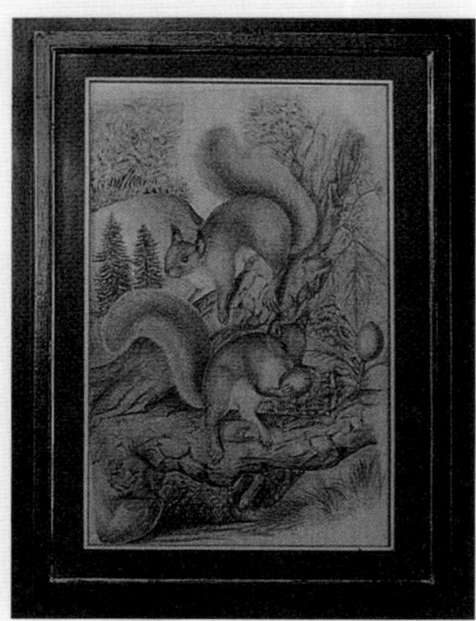

ADOLF DIETRICH, TWO SQUIRRELS, pencil
on paper, 18 x 11 ¹/₂" / ZWEI EICHHÖRNCHEN,
Bleistift auf Papier, 46 x 29 cm.
(PHOTO: RESTAURANT KRONENHALLE AG, ZÜRICH)

tations of identity and nation states. As I worked on my painting, my goal was to amplify those qualities which, in my mind, formed the basis of Dietrich's highly idiosyncratic construction of the real. While devising my composition, I followed Dietrich's use of elevated perspective, which allowed for a candid gaze upon the subject from high up in the trees and created an unmitigated relationship between viewer and subject. The goal was simply to put the "act of looking" and "nature" on the same footing.

TRAVEL

Since 2004, my fascination with Dietrich has continued to grow, and finally, a few months ago, when in preparation for writing the article you are currently reading, I decided it was time to pay a visit to Switzerland's Kunstmuseum Thurgau, home to one of the largest Dietrich collections in the world. Upon my arrival to the museum in Ittingen—having taken two trains, a bus, and walked a long distance down a country road to get there—I saw, in person for the first time, many of the paintings I'd previously only experienced as reproductions in books. Along with the extraordinary pieces being exhibited, I was fortunate enough to be taken by the museum's curator, Markus Landert, to see many of the works in the estate that were not on view—paintings, drawings, photographs, sketches, notes, and letters. This exposure to the depth of material in the archives entirely changed my perceptions of the artist. It made me see, for one, that Dietrich may not have been as much of an outsider as people thought (and still think), and that there may be another version of the events of his life that contradicts what we know of him and his art.

Walking into the gallery, I confronted two Dietrich portraits, one picturing him as a stern, elderly man, and another—much tougher in nature—of his elderly father. The dates of these two paintings and their subjects immediately revealed one misconception: that Dietrich didn't begin painting until late in life. In fact he completed his first paintings in 1902 at the age of twenty-five. I then began to focus on many of the other works installed around the gallery, thrilled by my first opportunity to see so many of Dietrich's strengths as an artist operating all at once and in full view. It occurred to me that one of Dietrich's most popular subjects—a local Bernese Mountain Dog named Balbo, who appears in many paintings—in many ways steals the show. The dog is simply more disarming (not to mention charming) than all of the other human portraits put together. In the famous GELBROTER ABENDHIMMEL (Yellow-Red Evening Sky, 1925), there is a luminous, orange sky amidst an array of unusual cloud and tree formations. The landscape is punctuated by a bunny running through the lushly painted foreground epitomizing the Rousseauian goals of the Neo-Romantic movement. The classic SCHIFFSSTEG IM WINTER (Boat Pier in Winter, 1940) opens onto a barren icescape with a decaying dock and a pair of swans—all articulated with Dietrich's typical complexity, highlighting a certain depth of emotion: what I might call his unique portrayal of deathly absence. As art historian Christoph Vögele wrote in 1994: "Dietrich saw his own living conditions mirrored in the seasonal bareness and coldness, abandonment and emptiness; his existen-

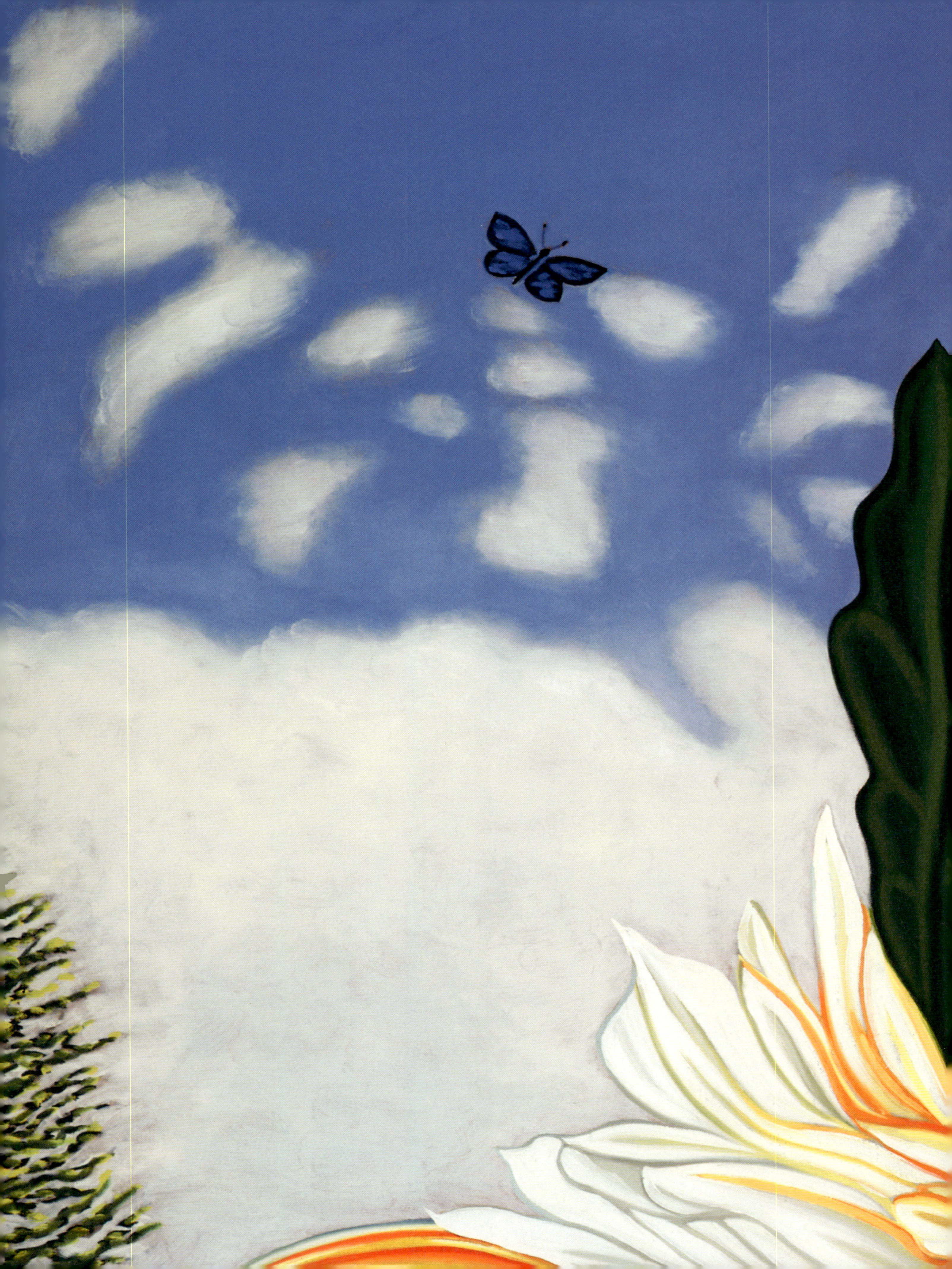

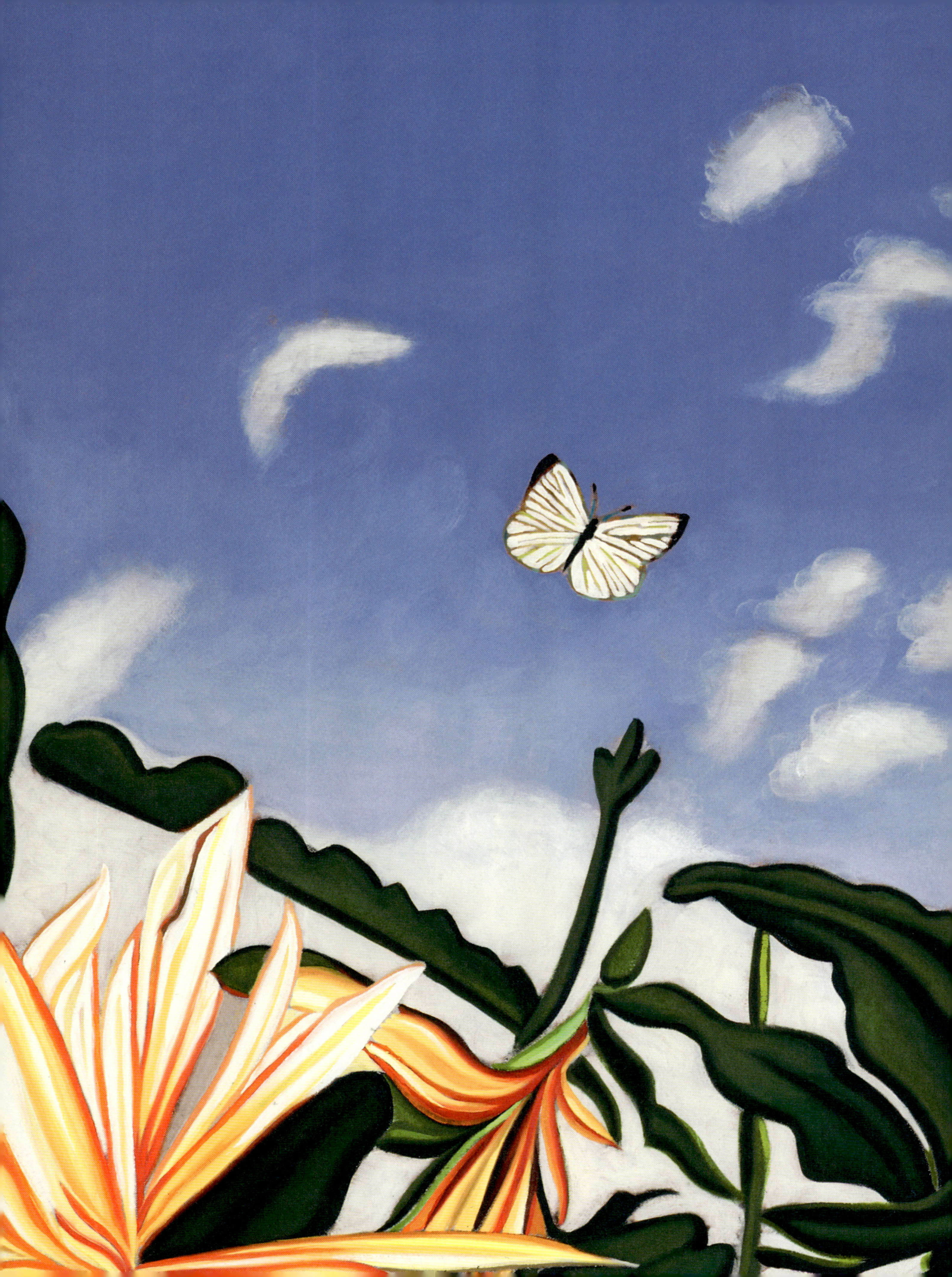

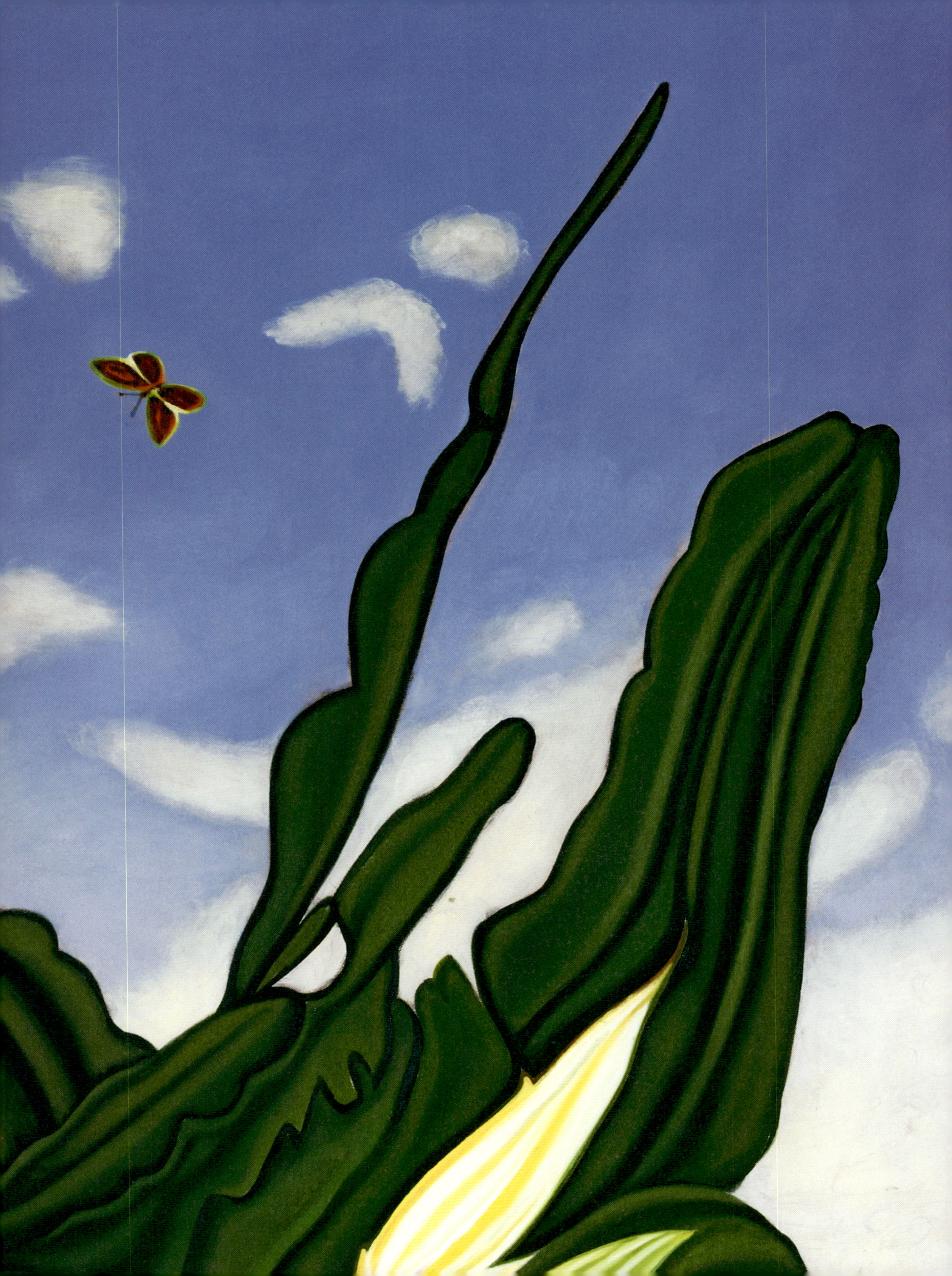

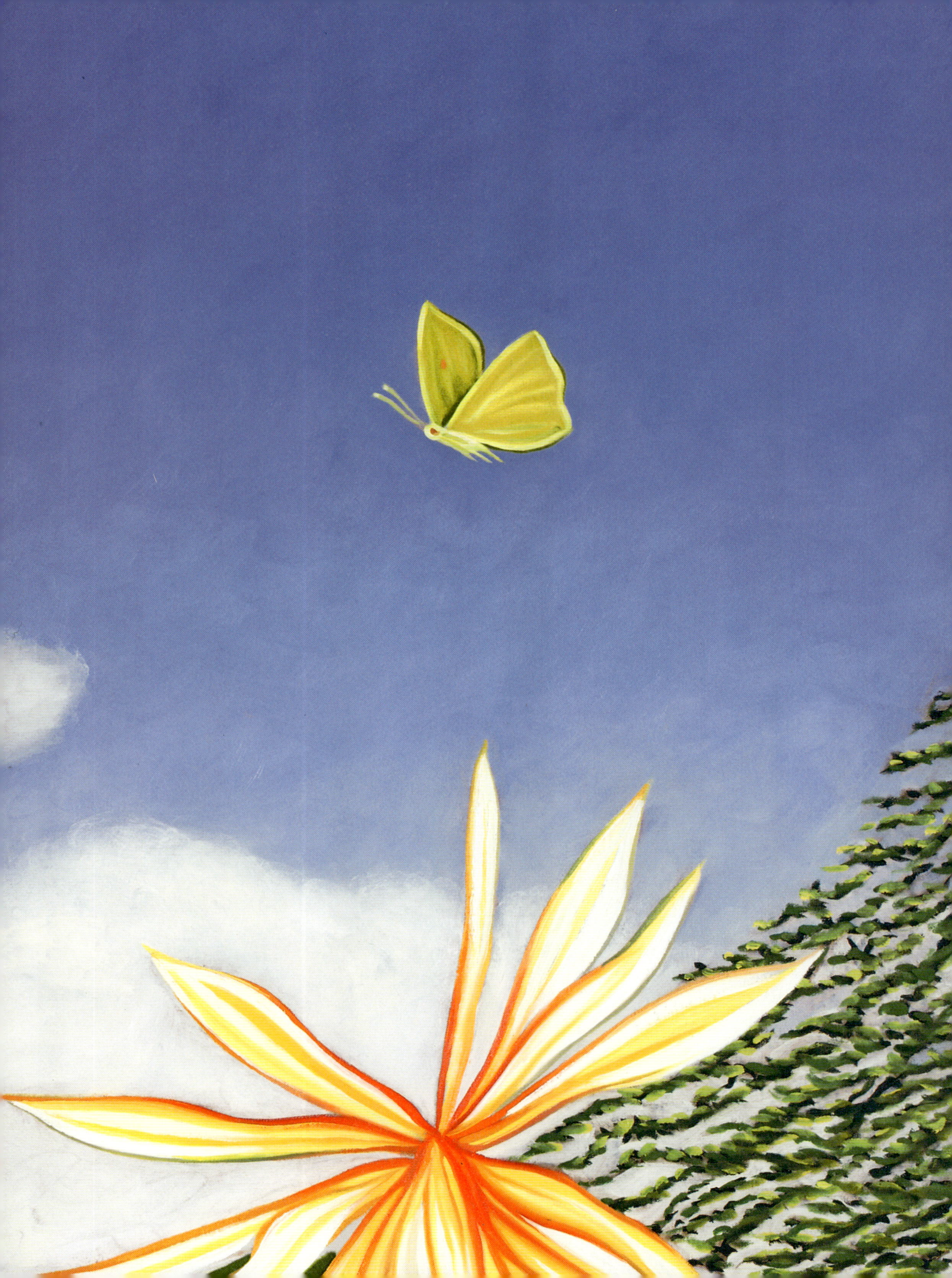

tial fears of poverty and war, his feelings of lone-liness."[1] After seeing this body of work in person, it was easy to understand how Dietrich came to be associated with the late-New Objectivism and Neo-Romantic movements.

Landert informed me that Dietrich was the youngest of four brothers and that he was from a very poor family. While his brothers left home seeking employment in larger towns and cities, Dietrich stayed in Berlingen to help support his parents, which meant running their small farm and tending to their single cow and goat. For additional income, he worked as a lumberjack and at a local textile mill. Nevertheless, he showed talent in his art and was encouraged by his elementary school teachers to pursue his artistic abilities. Looking at his earliest watercolors, one can see how committed he was to being taken seriously as an artist; he borrowed freely from popular publications, designing his own Nouveau Art borders in order to give them a "contemporary" look. Some of his earliest paintings combine still life imagery with romantic motifs. Their palettes are extremely saturated in hue and have remarkable intensity, as is the case with HERMELIN UND TOTE MÖWE IN MOND-SCHEINLANDSCHAFT (Ermine and Dead Seagull in Moonlight Landscape, 1908), a nocturne that pictures an ermine and a hanging bird.

I made an interesting discovery while comparing the front and back of many works, where I found clear evidence of the artist's poverty. His supplies must have been limited, forcing him to make use of all surfaces. In one work on paper, for example, there's a highly detailed rendering of a tiger (inspired by a trip to the zoo) with two disassociated landscapes drawn on the back of the same sheet. Early drawings—one of his father and another of a hare—reveal the artist's unusual sensitivity both in charcoal and chalk on toned paper. Pencil drawings likewise display his ability to create atmosphere, which he carried over to his paintings on cardboard and wood panel. Dietrich's sketchbooks show how extensive and relentless he was at recording all sorts of compositional ideas, as well as keeping detailed notes on color, time of day, and even weather—all of which facilitated his early Romantic works and his methodical transition to the "Swiss Picturesque."

Yet, along with his conventional painterly exploration, he also conducted more audacious experiments, such as allowing children to finish his drawings for him in order to capture their unselfconscious expressiveness. Dietrich never made paintings from these particular drawings (what if he had?), as he considered them finished works on their own, a kind of side project used to provide a playful critique to his more stable working method. Where he combined disparate, often contradictory aspects of his practice, he did so with specific, refined intentions. He brought together, for example, direct observation (usually still life) with the landscape notations he'd recorded in his sketchbooks. As Dietrich's colleague and fellow

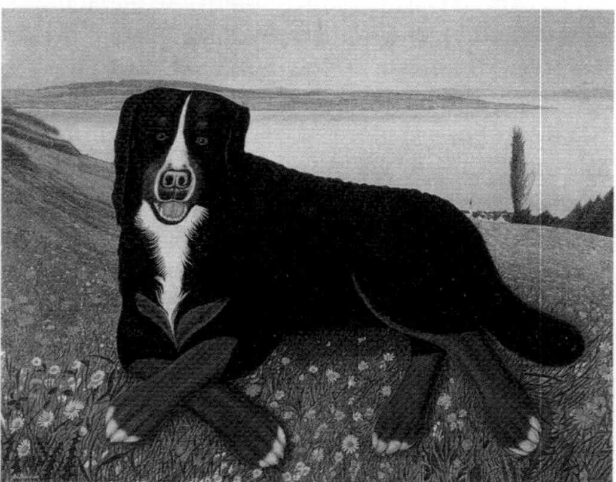

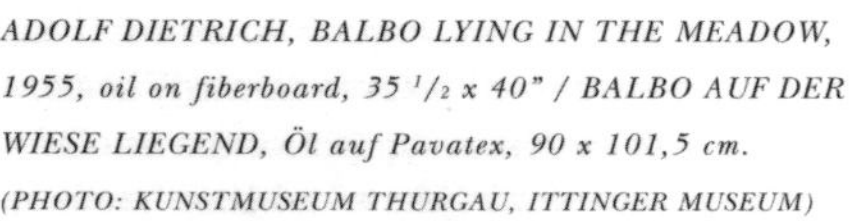
ADOLF DIETRICH, BALBO LYING IN THE MEADOW, 1955, oil on fiberboard, 35 1/2 x 40" / BALBO AUF DER WIESE LIEGEND, Öl auf Pavatex, 90 x 101,5 cm. (PHOTO: KUNSTMUSEUM THURGAU, ITTINGER MUSEUM)

1/12–4/12:
Richard Phillips
<u>Large Still Life (Queen of the Night)</u>
2010
111 x 108 in. / 281.9 x 274.3 cm
Oil on linen
Courtesy of the artist and
Gagosian Gallery, New York

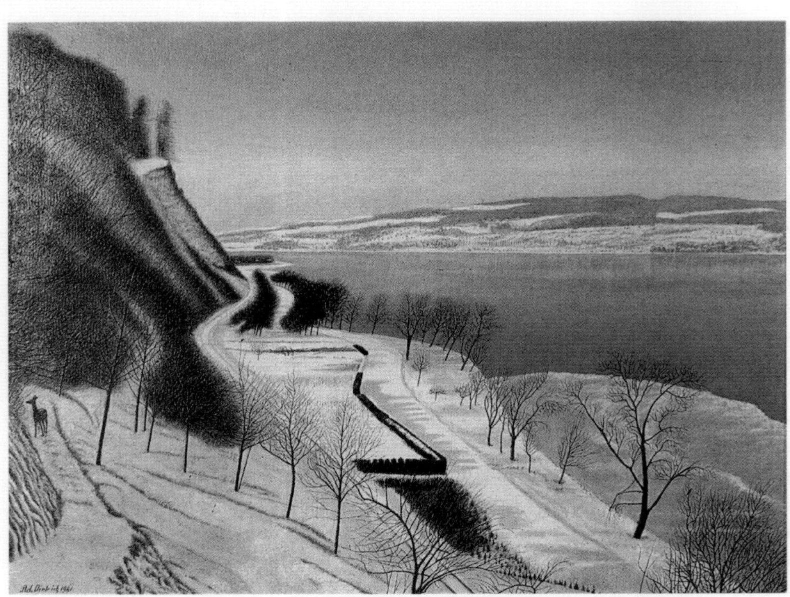

*ADOLF DIETRICH, WINTER AT LAKE CONSTANCE, 1941, oil on cardboard,
18 x 23 ¹/₂" / WINTER AM UNTERSEE, Öl auf Karton, 46 x 59,5 cm.
(PHOTO: KUNSTMUSEUM THURGAU, ITTINGER MUSEUM)*

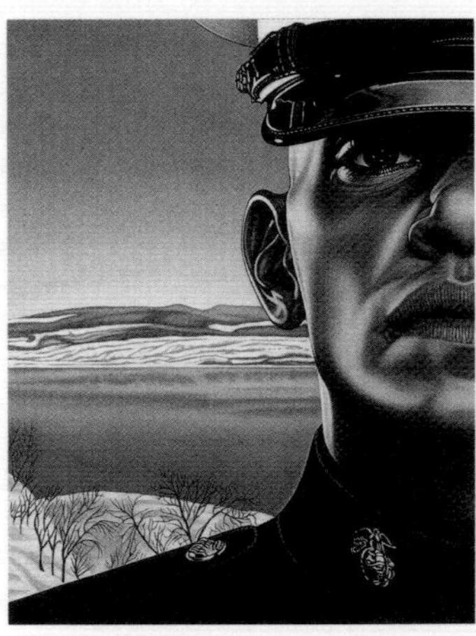

*RICHARD PHILLIPS, MESSAGE FORCE
MULTIPLIER, 2009, oil on canvas,
78 x 58 ¹/₂" / MEINUNGSVERSTÄRKER,
Öl auf Leinwand, 198,1 x 148,6 cm.
(PHOTO: GAGOSIAN GALLERY, NEW YORK)*

New Objective painter Georg Schrimpf said in reference to their similar working process: "Although I draw the composition of a landscape outside with a few strokes in a sketchbook, I paint the oil paintings later when I'm alone and everything is quiet around me; I don't merely paint the landscape I see, but the landscape that I see inside me."[2]

ART WORLD

Around the year 1916, Dietrich was discovered by the German art dealer Herbert Tannenbaum, who represented the artist until 1937 when he had to flee the Nazis. Sales made during these years led to a period of modest prosperity for Dietrich, allowing him to make a major acquisition—a camera—that wound up having a significant effect on his working process for the rest of his career. The use of photography galvanized Dietrich's commitment to the pic-

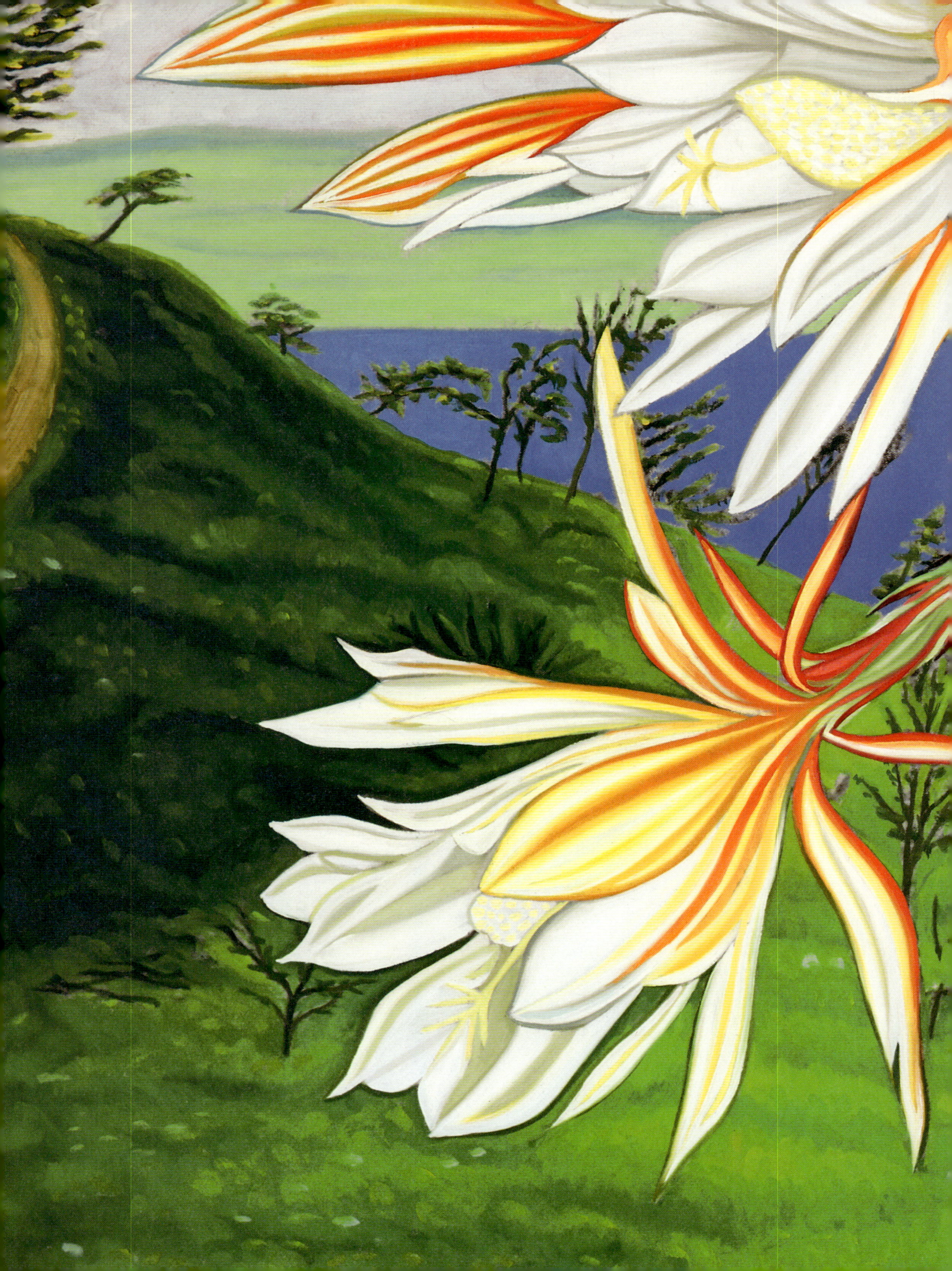

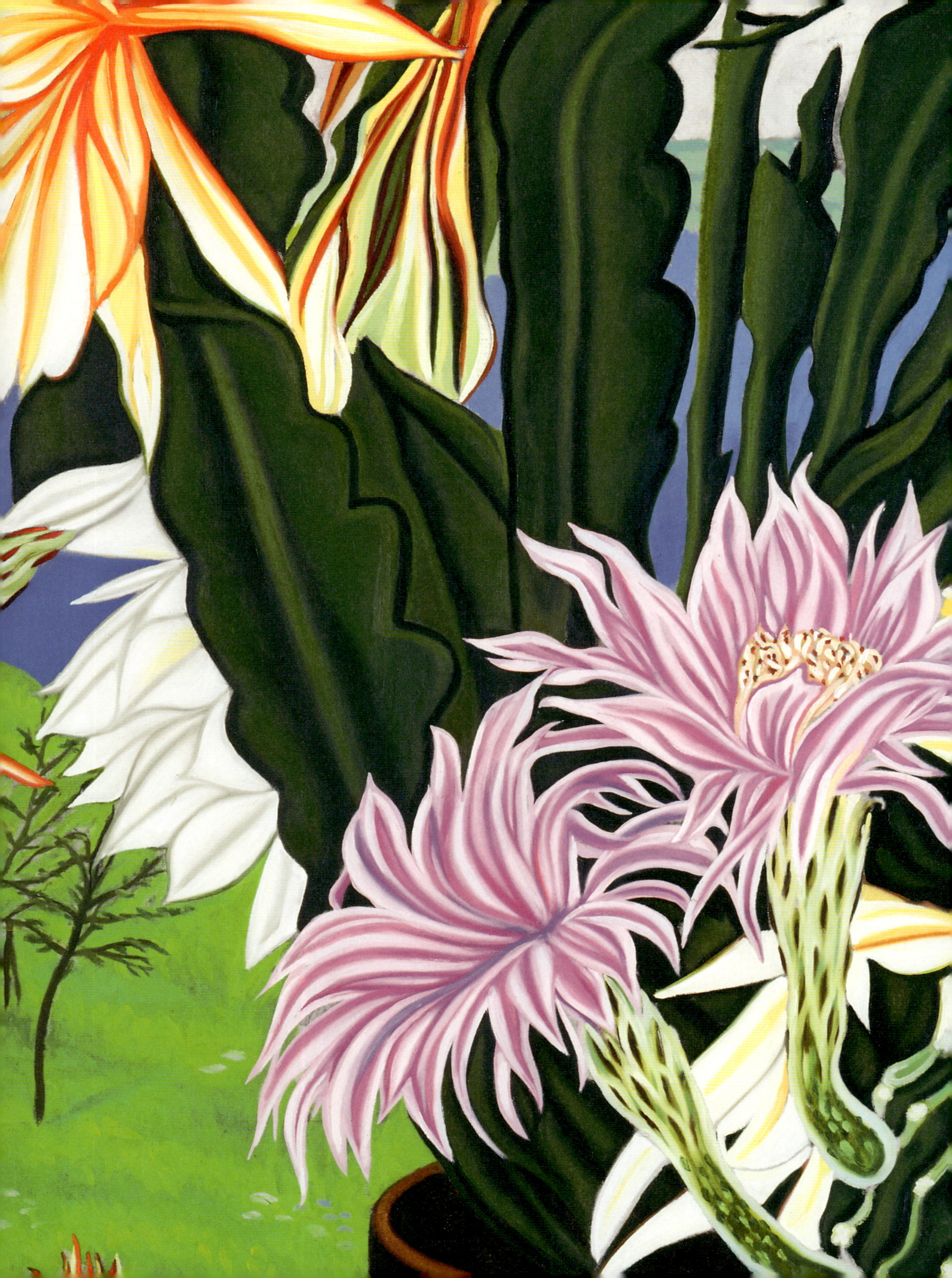

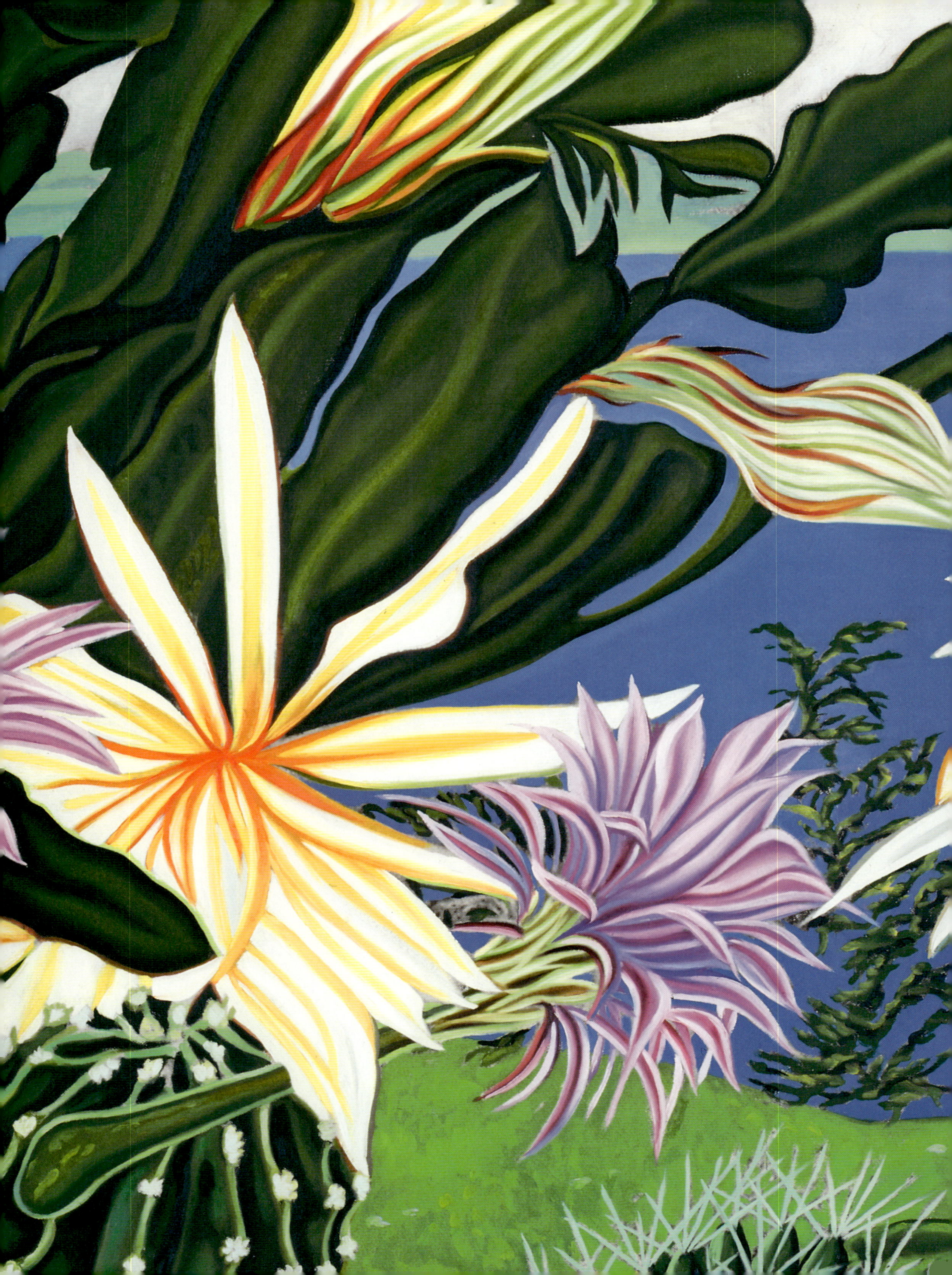

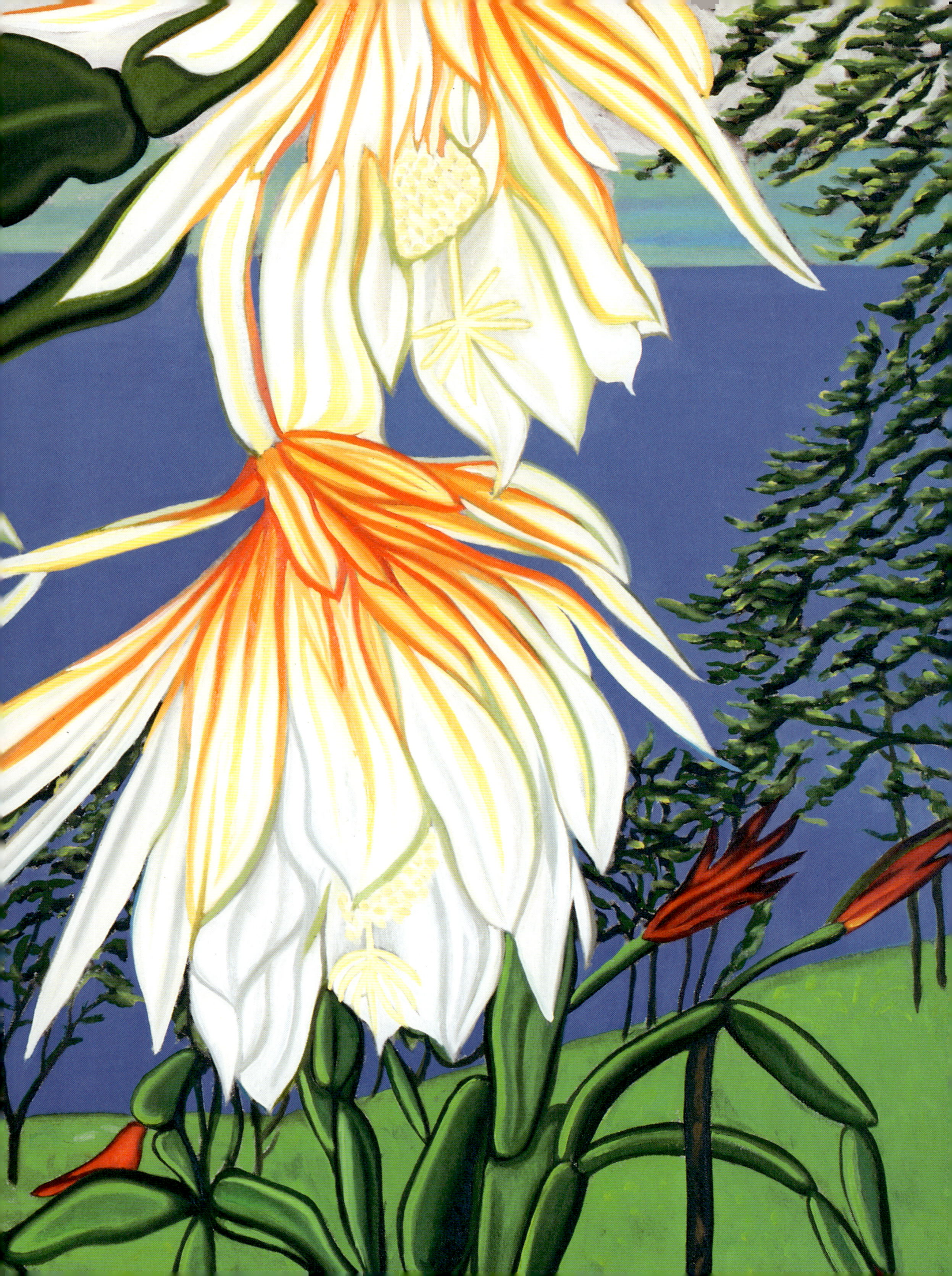

turesque and to the process of recording subtle shifts in atmosphere.

Together with his notational sketches, the small black-and-white photos he took became further tools for refining his imagery. This led to the production of a few extremely detailed, photo-realistic paintings, including a portrait of a toucan titled, PFEFFER-VOGEL (Toucan, 1927), and a still life of taxidermied ducks called GROSSES STILLLEBEN MIT ENTEN, EIS-VÖGELN UND FISCHEN (Large Still Life with Ducks, Kingfishers, and Fish, 1925). He also created larger and more complex drawings, which he then transfer-red onto cardboard or panel and traced repeatedly until they were entirely worn out.

The medium of photography also played a part in Tannenbaum's effort to introduce Dietrich's work—to "campaign" him, so to speak—to a broader audi-ence. Part of this involved showing his work to Franz Roh, who immediately championed Dietrich, refer-ring to him as a kind of naïve realist, and thus the embodiment of the ideals of New Objectivity and the Post-/Anti-Expressionist movement. In 1925, Diet-rich's work was included in an exhibition of New Ob-jective artists at the Kunsthalle in Mannheim: "Neue Sachlichkeit: Deutsche Maler nach dem Expressio-nismus" (New Objectivity: German Painters after Expressionism). It was then that Tannenbaum and Roh hatched a scheme to promote Dietrich as the New Objectivity's "Rustic" Rousseau. A photographer was immediately sent to Berlingen to begin the myth-building process by staging the artist in a variety of tableaus all of which portrayed him as a hermit liv-ing in the forest and painting in a small dilapidated woodshed. Misleading photos were also taken of the artist painting outdoors, which he did do but only ra-rely. He was fictitiously cast as a man entirely isolated from society, when, in fact, he was quite socially ac-tive, living in the center of Berlingen's square, where he was keenly aware of daily town life from the perch of his front window. He also welcomed and regularly entertained visitors, who occasionally commissioned him to paint their portraits. The odd, un-modulated, flat lighting of the portraits is due to the fact that he worked from photographs of his sitters.

Contrary to any portrayal of him as an unsophis-ticated "outsider" artist, Dietrich was a consummate technician and was always devising new ways of im-proving his painting and achieving specific visual effects in certain works. Yet, social interaction espe-cially of an intimate nature was difficult for Dietrich, who never married. It can be noted in reading his correspondence that he employed a dating service to help introduce him to women, but to no avail. Sig-nificantly, many of the views that he favored for his paintings were also the sites he considered to be most romantically enticing. His efforts in matters of love and intimacy, even while unrequited, further dispel the myth of him as a "loner" intentionally withdrawn from society. Dietrich also happened to be a proli-fic writer; he wrote more than a thousand letters to friends and admirers of his work.

He is known to have ridden on the back of a friend's motorcycle to Munich—one of his few trips out of Berlingen—where he made a pilgrimage to the Alte Pinakothek to see paintings by Albrecht Dürer. These paintings inspired him to make tech-nically stronger work. Upon his return from Munich, he is said to have invited painters to visit his studio, at which point he asked them, flat out, for advice on how he could improve his methods. With this advice and inspiration his interior world grew exponentially. While, geographically speaking, he was somewhat provincial, his openness, curiosity, social ambitions, and eagerness to achieve technical mastery made him the direct opposite of a naïve/romantic/rustic outsider artist. If anything he was technological, ap-propriative, innovative, and thus a parallel-modern (though in a more rustic way), which clearly distingu-ishes him from the metropolitan or at least urban ar-tist culture. His fascination with animals, botany, and atmosphere led to a mode of pictorial representation that was totally animated, if not hyper-animated.

Dietrich developed the ability to use his various sources and techniques to completely synthesize the real. This took him far beyond the painterly mode of careful observation while giving him means to evade strict abstraction. The radicality of his vision might thus be seen as a reinterpretation of the constituent forms of representation for the purpose of creating an advanced emotional and physical connection to places and things. It allowed him to invest sites and animals with an internal realism, animating them from within and psychologically expanding them beyond what we see on the surface.

The efforts of Roh and Tannenbaum to falsify Dietrich in a way that would bolster his marketability did result in short-term financial gain, but had the lasting effect of severely marginalizing and limiting our access to one of the most important artists of his generation. As a Swiss national treasure he remains to this day a kind of enigma. When Tannenbaum was forced to flee Europe, Dietrich's active relationship with his exploitative dealer abruptly ended although Tannenbaum was able to continue selling the work during the war, thus maintaining the positive and negative effect he was having on the artist.

MECHANIZED WAR

Following World War I, realism in painting split into two camps, or coalesced around two different positions. There was New Objectivity with its pessimism and alienation, and post-expressionist tendencies, which were in favor of an un-idealized representation of the failure of the Enlightenment. Then there was Neo-Romanticism, which turned away from industrial society and represented a nature made vulnerable by the onset of human treachery, a nature seen slipping away. The idealization of the landscape through naïve and neo-primitive styles drifted toward a conservative style that was eventually appropriated by the Nazis and used for propaganda as in Dietrich's inclusion in *NS Frauenwarte*, September 1937, a Nazi lifestyle magazine for women.

The relationship Dietrich's paintings had to either of these concepts is dubious, as he was not a polemical or ideological theoretician; while he was aware of some of the artists involved, he claimed in letters to have no use for them. Instead of using his observations and constructions as a way to communicate the obvious turmoil in society, and thus succumbing to one of the predominant discourses, he used his detailed representation of nature to stabilize the act of looking so that experiencing his art would evoke sustainable emotional and psychological responses beyond that of formal gestures.

The relative simplicity of his auto-didactic work was therefore an alternative to the didacticism of an over-strategized, synthetic formalism. In retrospect, Dietrich's art can be seen to have been paradoxically built i n t o and o u t o f Weimar art history. While it was made in a rural setting and in the midst of great hardship, Dietrich's art is still a giant achievement of modern art from that time and was only, in fact, marginalized by the efforts of a few. When removed from the context of false mythologies and commercial ploys, the paintings themselves hold the truth of their own making and of a lost thread in modernity. They are neither centered on negotiation with projected future styles nor are they a tactical reprisal of previous genres. Nevertheless, Dietrich strove to make a connection with his audience using a combination of science (photography), media (tourist brochures and magazines), observation (sketches and notations), and technique.

Dietrich's intense focus on the vicissitudes of contemporary life in Berlingen and the deliberate autonomy of his style offer an alternative to the version of events in a hierarchically perceived history of modern art that we have grown accustomed to and accept as fact.

In the wake of World War II and the clash between the aesthetics of expressionism and abstraction— the binary opposition of expressionism and abstraction—the "representational image" was thought of as either reactionary or the result of misplaced propaganda. But the experience of looking at a Dietrich painting in person refutes this fiction outright while illuminating the underpinnings of an alternative reading of history. When I went to Ittingen to see Dietrich's paintings, I had a strong sense that I was independently mending something that had been tethered—tying back together the experience that had been thoroughly cut apart by forces entirely outside the art.

Art professionals with their conduit to history have misappropriated the work of Dietrich, thereby succeeding in being conventionally wrong. When I reached the museum in Ittingen and stood in front the paintings, I knew that it was the exact opposite: that Dietrich, if anything, had been unconventionally right.

1) Christoph Vögele, "Landschaft" in *Adolf Dietrich und die Neue Sachlichkeit in Deutschland* (Winterthur: Kunstmuseum, 1994; Oldenburg: Landesmuseum, 1995), p. 69.
2) Ibid., p. 73.

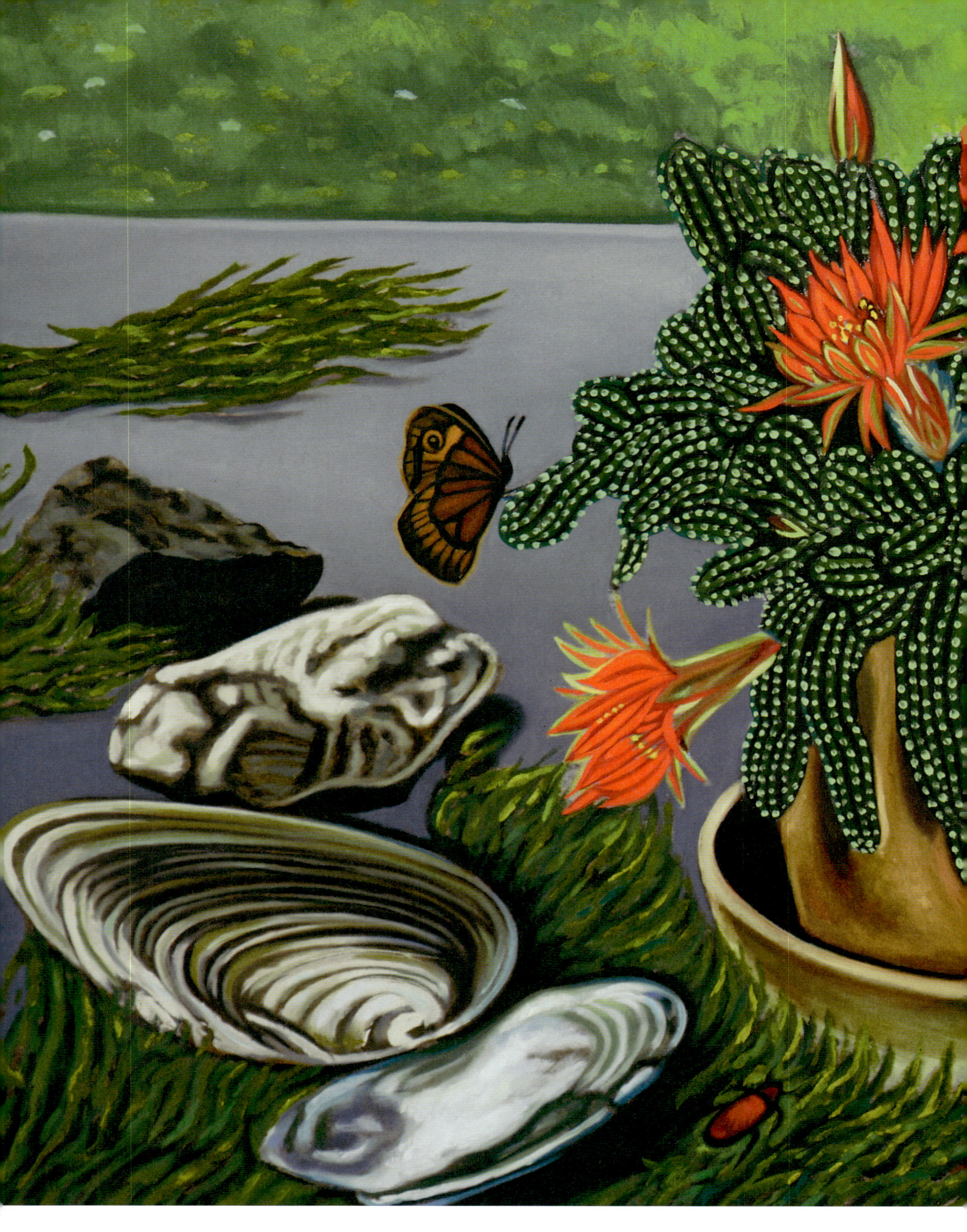

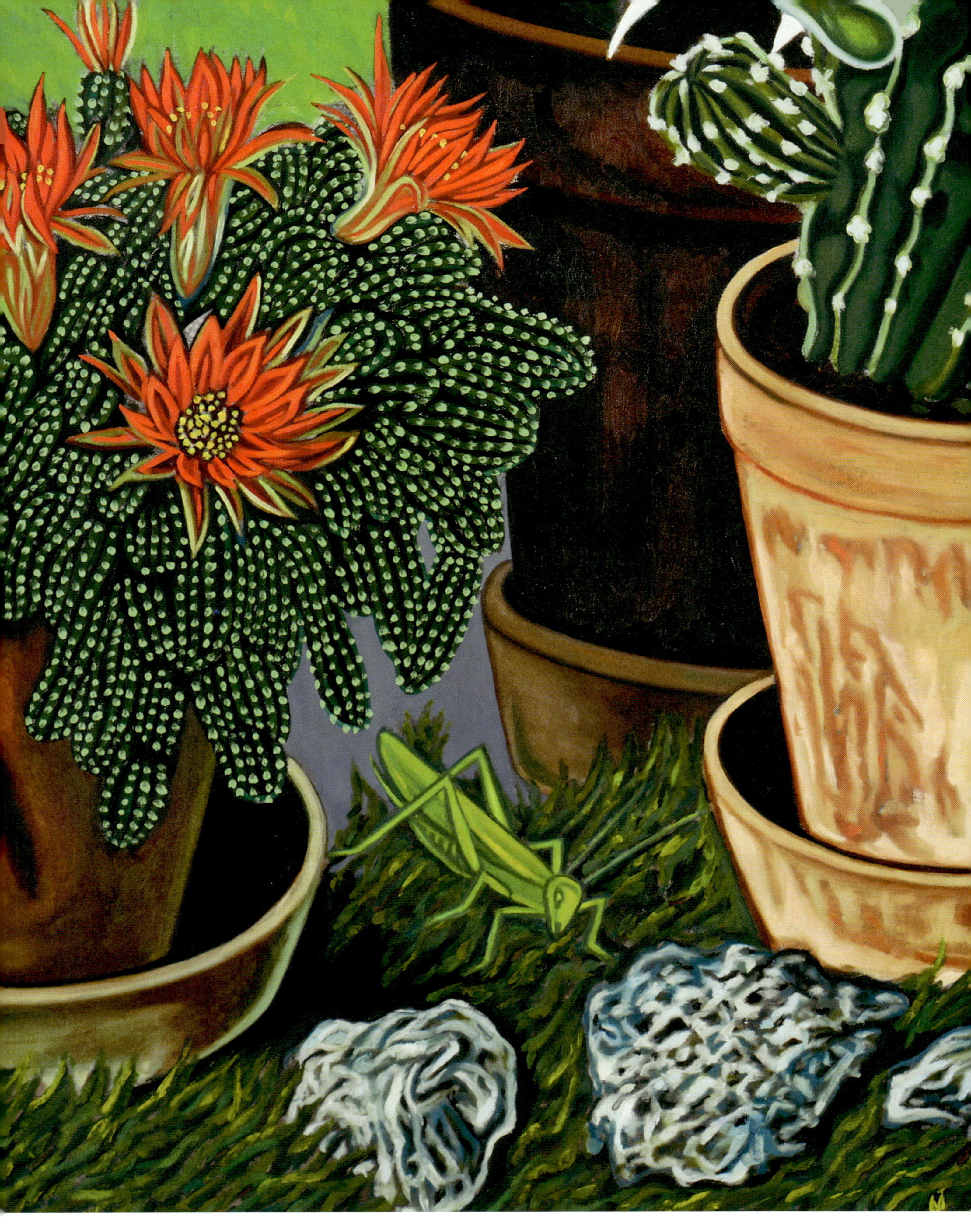

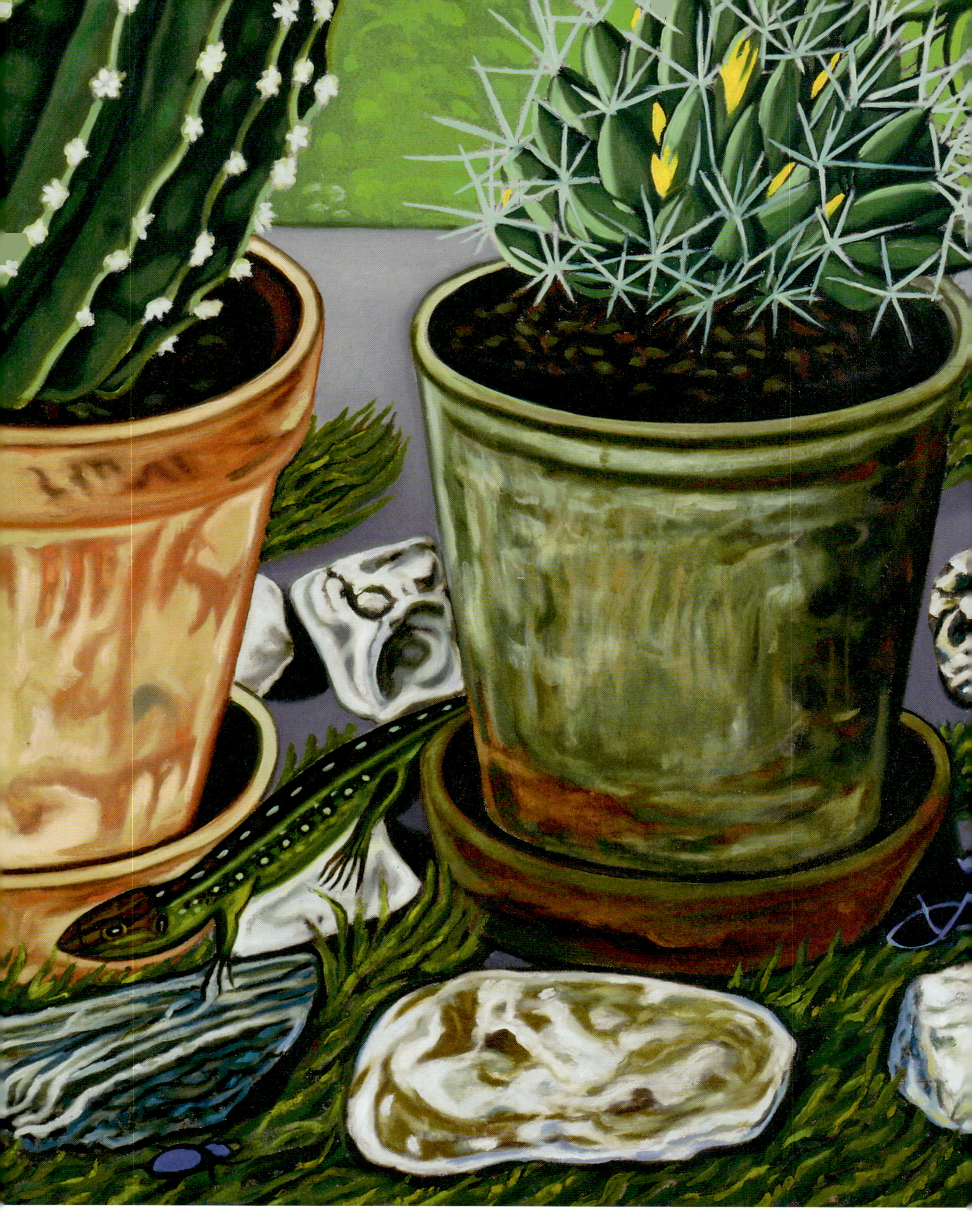

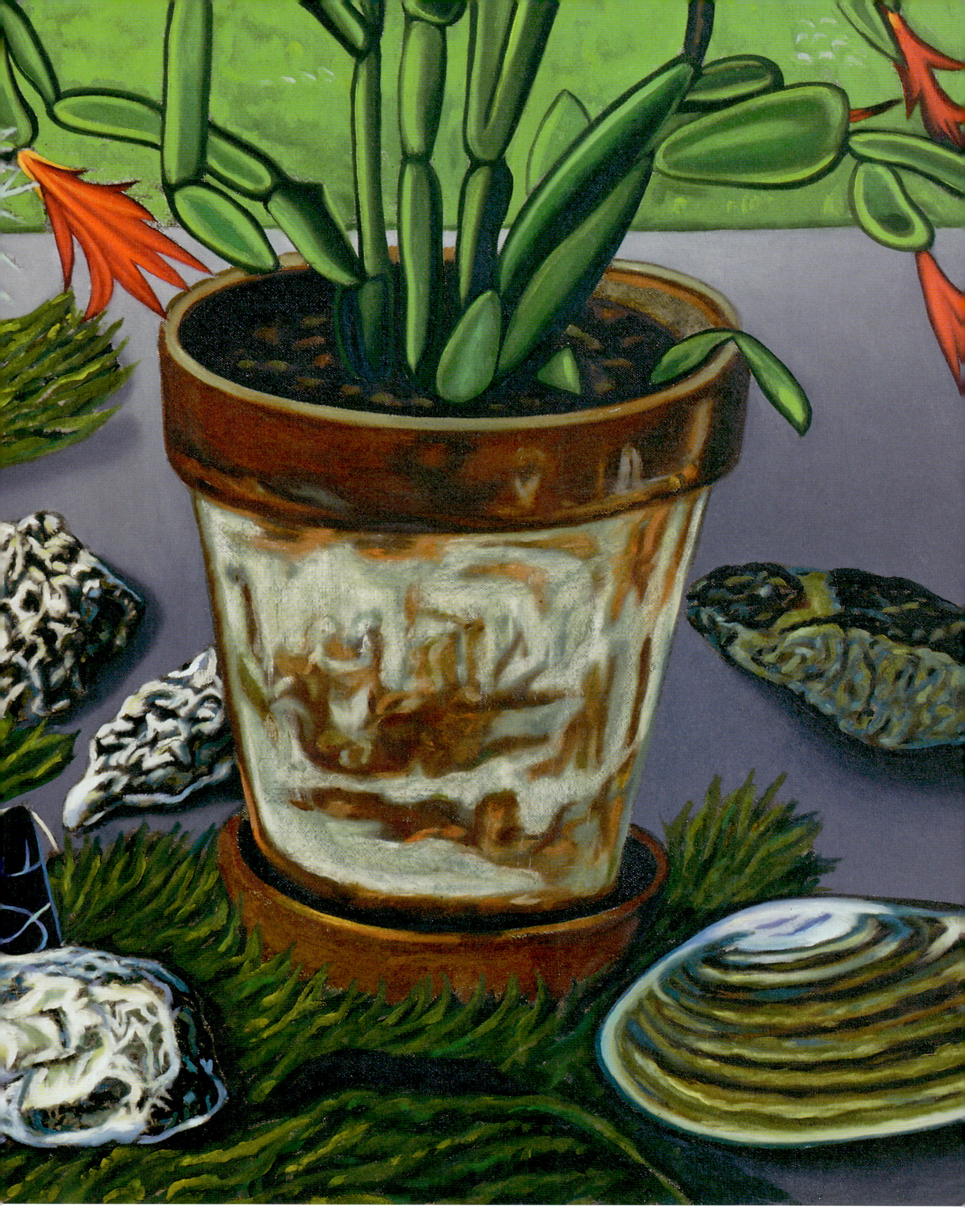

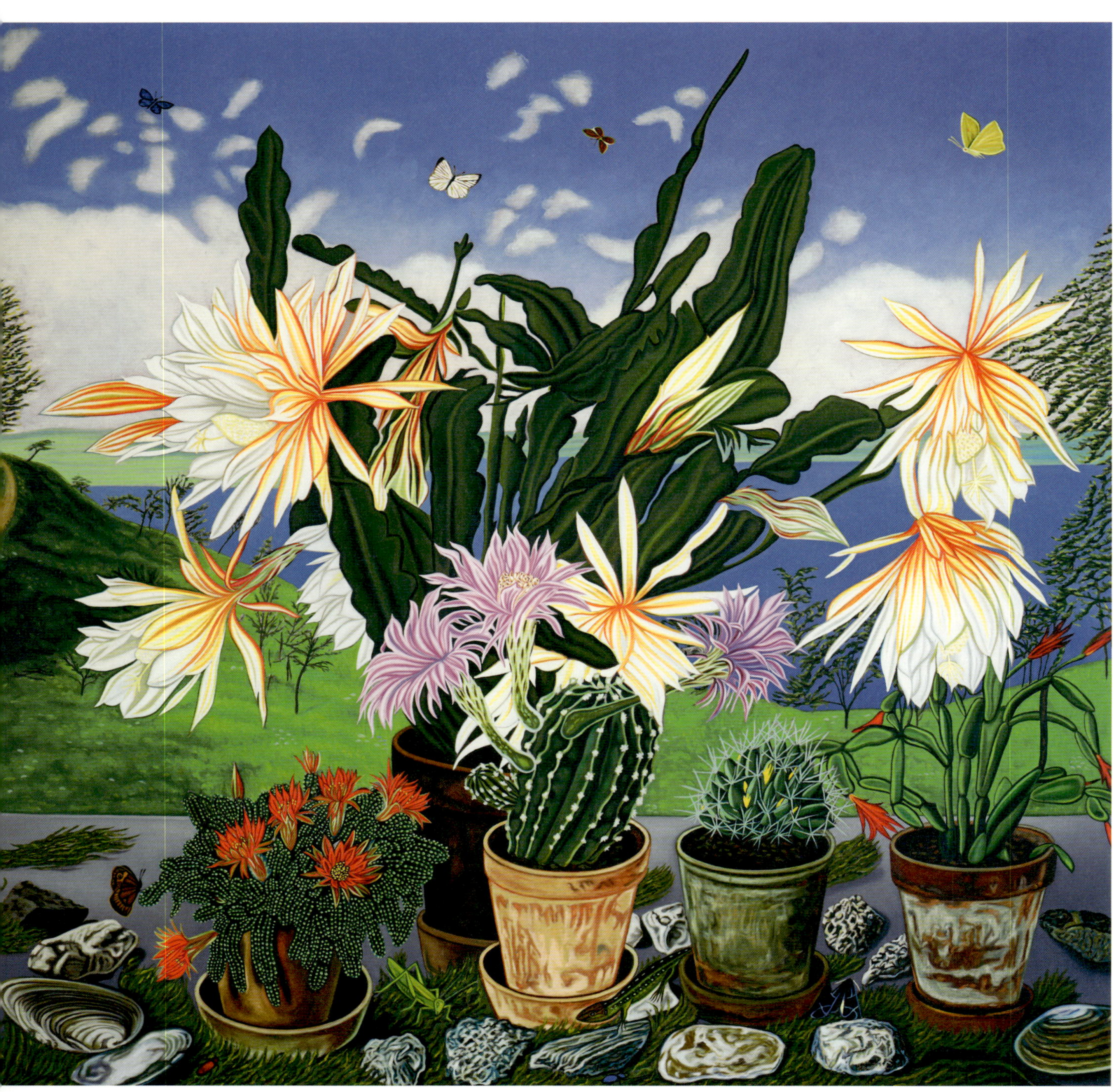

9/12–12/12 and Left–right:
Richard Phillips
Large Still Life (Queen of the Night)
2010
111 x 108 in. / 281.9 x 274.3 cm
Oil on linen
Courtesy of the artist and
Gagosian Gallery, New York

Adolf Dietrich
Blühende Kakteen vor Landschaft
1941
30.3 x 31.5 in. / 77 x 80 cm
Oil on plywood
Private collection, Beverly Hills

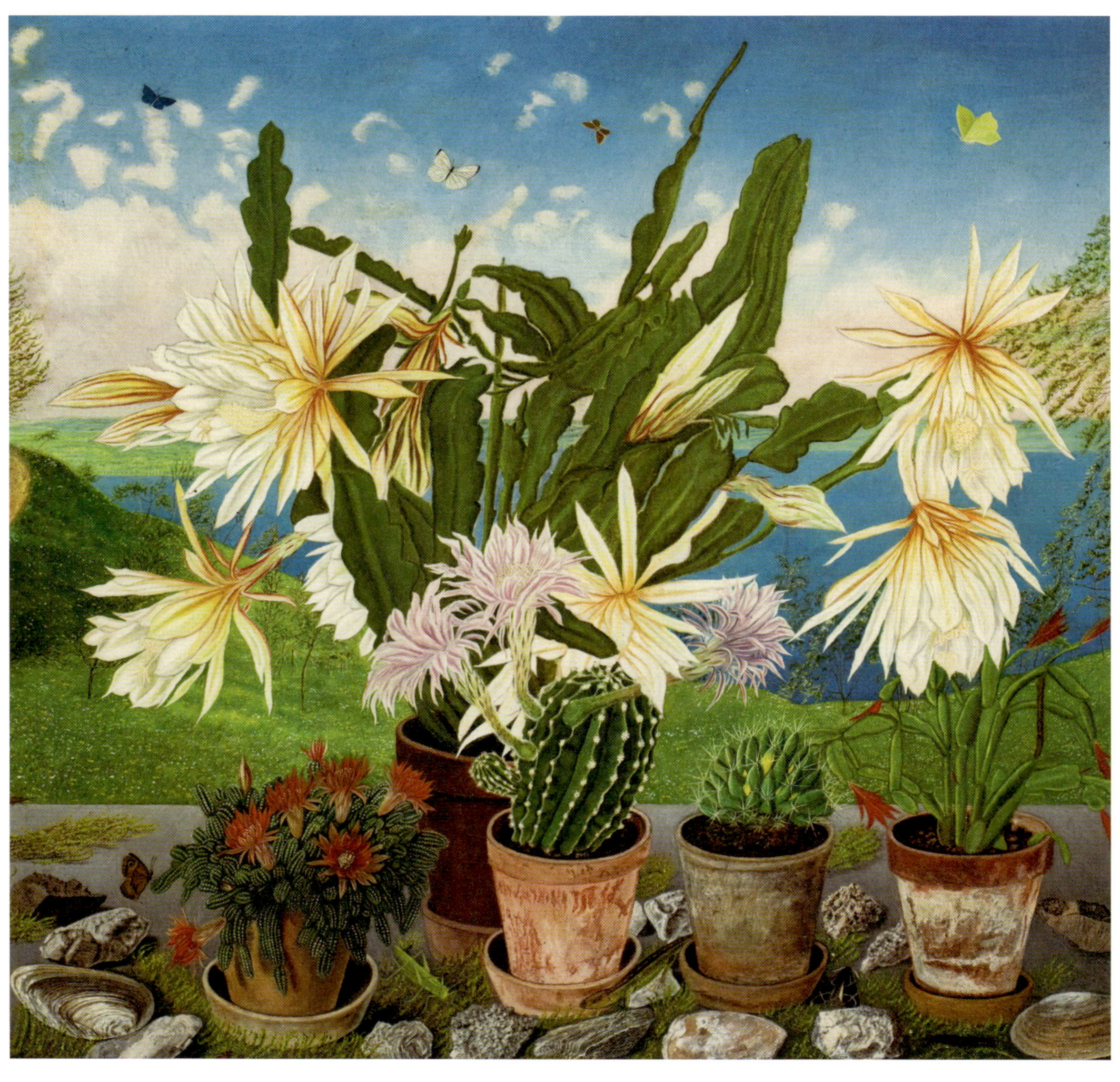

Adolf Dietrich
<u>Grüner See</u>
1932
11.3 x 23.2 in. / 28.8 x 33.3 cm
Oil on cardboard
Private collection, Kristina Wyss-Böhni

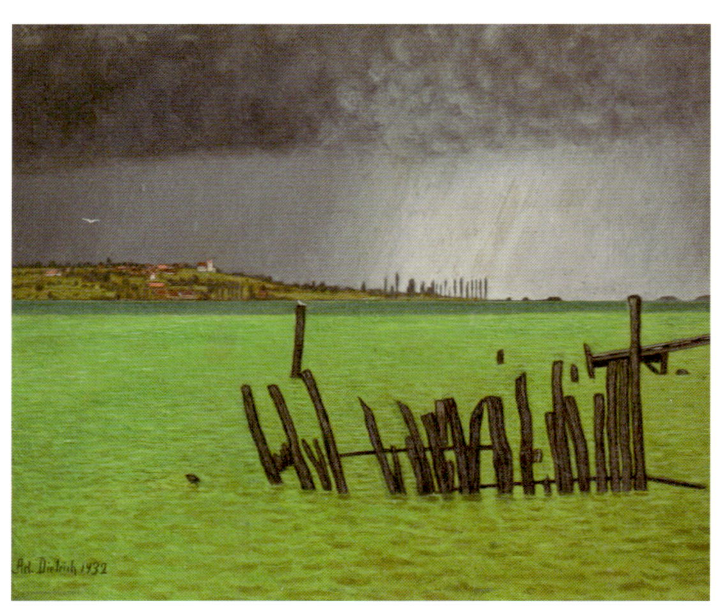

Adolf Dietrich
<u>Nachbargärtchen im Frühling</u>
1939
21.7 x 16.4 in. / 55 x 41.7 cm
Oil on cardboard
Kunstmuseum des Kantons Thurgau,
Ittinger Museum

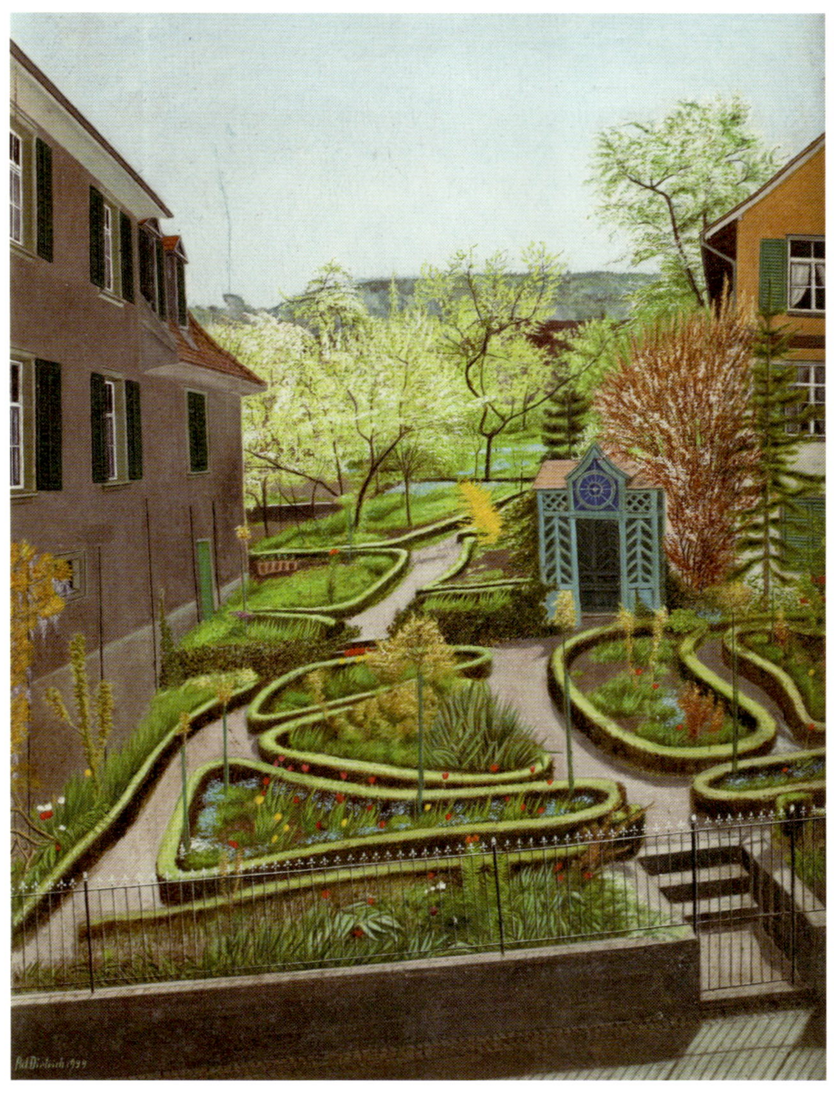

Adolf Dietrich
<u>Kaninchen und Aquarium</u>
1939
11.6 x 9.1 in. / 29.5 x 23 cm
Oil on cardboard
Private collection

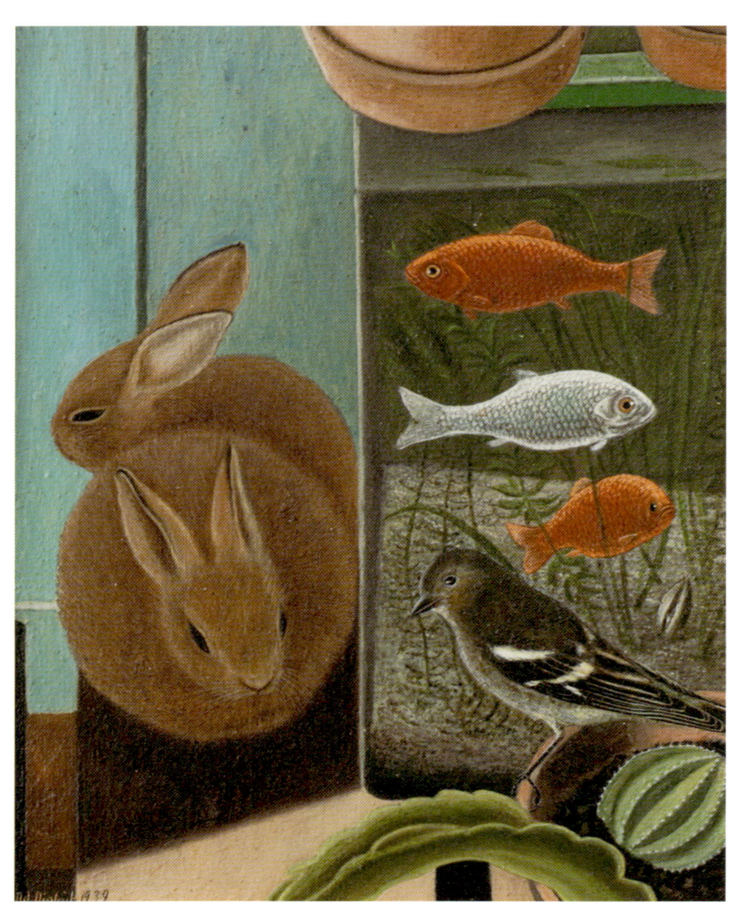

Adolf Dietrich
<u>Pfeffervogel</u>
1927
18.1 x 15 in. / 46 x 38 cm
Oil on cardboard
Städtische Museen Konstanz

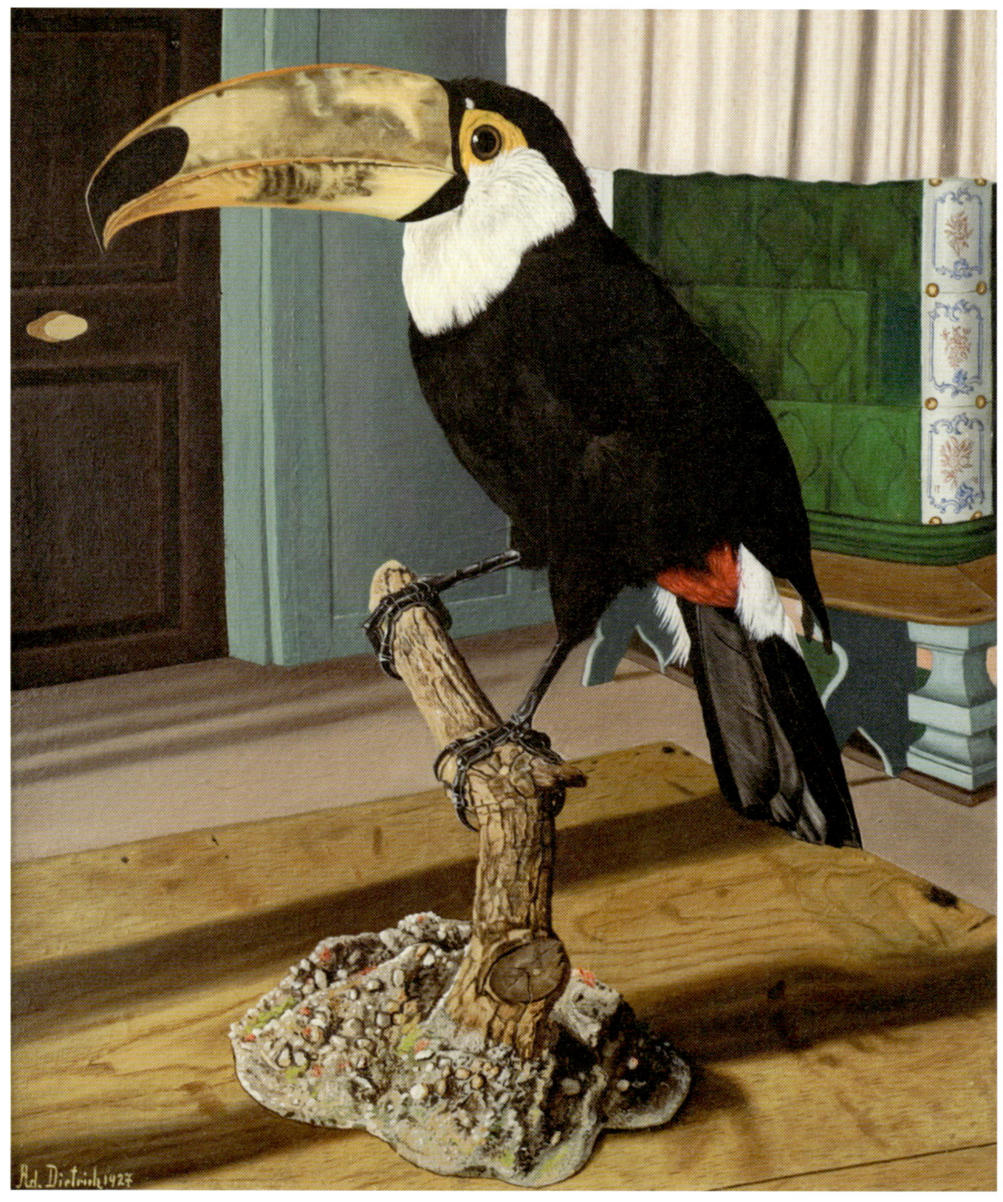

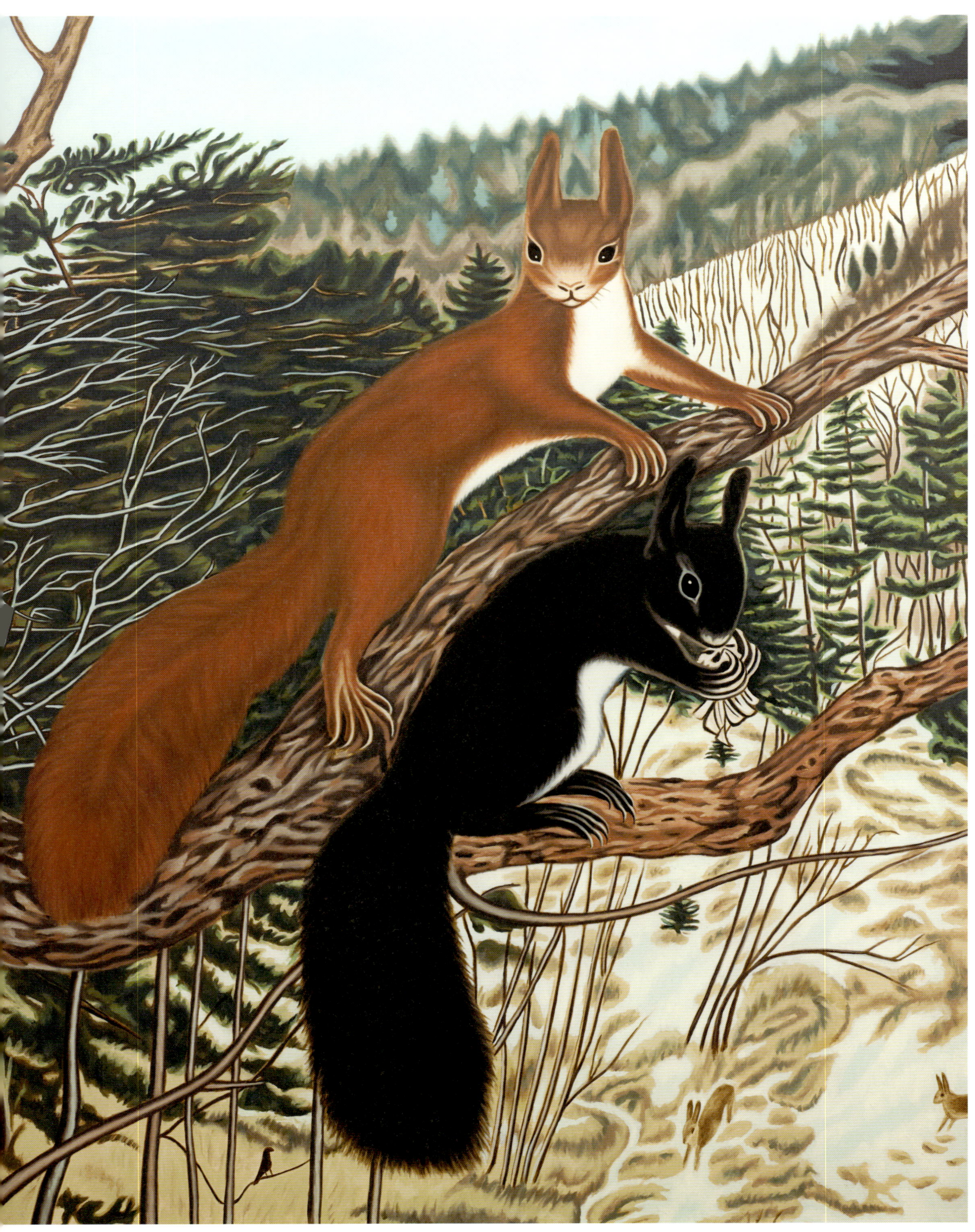

Left–right:
Richard Phillips
Similar to Squirrels (after A. Dietrich)
2003
102.5 x 78 in. / 260.4 x 198.1 cm
Oil on linen
Hall Collection

Adolf Dietrich
Eichhörnchenbild / Zwei Eichhörnchen
in Landschaft
1939
24.4 x 17.1 in. / 62 x 43.5 cm
Oil on cardboard
Private collection

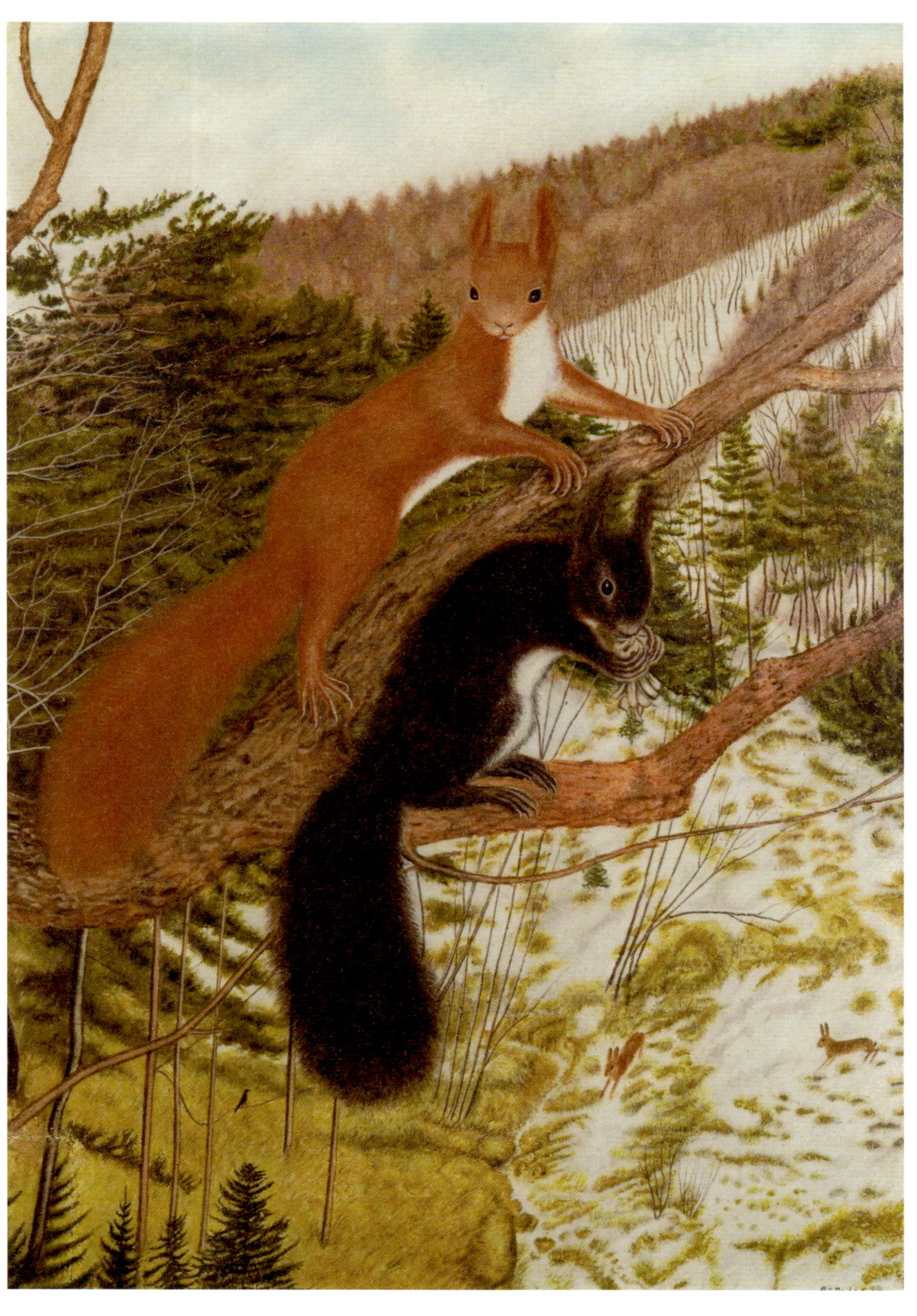

IN

CONVERSATION

BEATRIX RUF AND RICHARD PHILLIPS

BEATRIX RUF:
When did your fascination with Adolf Dietrich begin?
RICHARD PHILLIPS:
It started in 2003, when I was visiting Zurich. After a dinner at the Kronenhalle, Peter Fischli took me to see a specific work in the restaurant's formidable collection. We walked upstairs to see a drawing of two squirrels in a tree by Adolf Dietrich, who, Peter explained, was an artist considered to be a Swiss national treasure.

Compared to the modern paintings within the collection, the drawing seemed to me to connect more to contemporary art than it did to historical drawing. When I received the catalogue raisonné from you, I discovered that the text was entirely in German. While looking at the photographs and the pictures, and not being too careful about the dates, I assumed that Dietrich only started painting when he was in his seventies, and that he was a self-taught, naïve artist. So after a while, I convinced myself of that story. Later I came to learn that he did indeed go to school, and that his teachers noticed his aptitude for drawing and encouraged it, but that the extreme poverty in which he grew up with his parents meant that he couldn't give himself over full-time to making art until later in life.

BEATRIX RUF:
Adolf Dietrich's art-historical categorization indeed leans toward the "naïve"—and was very much influenced, distorted even, by historical and political circumstances, as you can see in his exhibition history, his presence in international shows in the context of the *Neue Sachlichkeit* early on, and the reversal of this international presence through the politics of the Nazis.

Dietrich also evokes "pragmatisms" one often finds in the so-called naïve, but upon closer inspection, his drawings, photographs, and the techniques of montage and variations he developed and used for his paintings reveal another story. Dietrich was also a master of self-mythologizing, which is a signifier not only for the naïve artist, but for the artist in general. There is this wonderful quote from Dietrich: "When I was twenty-six, I saw a tourist in Berlingen, [Switzerland], painting a seascape and I thought that I also could do that. At home I took a piece of cardboard and a few tubes of paint. The experiment succeeded, and since then people from all over the world have visited, telling me my paintings are beautiful". And he signed his paintings like Albrecht Dürer: A. D.

RICHARD PHILLIPS:
What's interesting to me is just how deliberate he was in his practice, in using photographs, in drawing, in planning paintings. His production was quite traditional on one hand, but he was also very much involved with thinking about his market in what seems to be a contemporary manner. As such, he was aware of the production of his own naïveté. Some considered him to be the Henri Rousseau of the *Neue Sachlichkeit*. But when painters visited him, he would quiz them quite closely about their methods, so that he could produce more complex paintings. None of the *Neue Sachlichkeit* painters were reaching that level of so-called photo-real presentation. And yet, there is no ironic distancing in his works, as in the drawing of the squirrels. Similarly, I will also say that in my own work, I'm not making ironic gestures toward the reproduction of the naïve artist whatsoever. When my squirrel painting appeared for the first time, it seemed like a strong non sequitur, like, "What could possibly be meant by this, now that we have this painting of two squirrels?" My intention was to point my painting toward that state of mind and that type of effort as the subject matter, just as much as any subject matter, in the same way that one of my previous works could have pointed toward the subject of a photograph.

BEATRIX RUF:
In some of your works on view, you appropriate elements of landscapes from Dietrich paintings. Can you talk about the very emotional, even content-loaded images you use of Lake Constance in the late 1930s and '40s?

RICHARD PHILLIPS:
I wanted to use the landscapes as a psychological influence on the images I selected from the media that I had chosen to paint, specifically in two paintings, <u>Der Bodensee</u> [2008], and <u>Message Force Multiplier</u> [2009]. In each case, it was the same landscape of Lake Constance, seen from an aerial perspective. In <u>Der Bodensee</u>, which was taken from a pornographic image found on the web, the woman's heated-looking face is placed in the context of a frozen landscape, setting up a kind of dichotomy. For <u>Message Force Multiplier</u>, I chose an image of a marine recruitment advertisement meant to inspire young men to join today's military. The relationship to Dietrich's painting, its title, the proportion of landscape to proportion of figure, all had to do with a recombination of elements designed to undo the original intention of the advertisement, which was the creation of a staged falsehood of heroism and valor expressing the seriousness of military enlistment. So it refers to a doubling and redoubling of subjectivity, while putting the figure into and out of context, in order to try to shift and manipulate meaning.

BEATRIX RUF:
In some paintings, you completely appropriate images, and in some you just use them as backgrounds—a practice that reminds me of Dietrich's own use of image elements for variations of paintings.

RICHARD PHILLIPS:
The large still-life painting titled <u>Large Still Life (Queen of the Night)</u> [2010] and the painting <u>Similar to Squirrels</u> [2003] are complete appropriations. In the case of the still life, it's a portrait of night-blooming flowers seen in the daytime, a simple contradiction that Dietrich set up.

In each of the paintings where I'm using the landscapes, the whole idea of distortion and the construction of misunderstandings, or the deliberate destabilization of meaning, are all a part of the language that I use within my work to emphasize how our communications systems use information and misinformation to control and manipulate people.

BEATRIX RUF:
And there is criticism sometimes of your work not being in control of the manipulative use of seduction you of course use consciously and with critical distance in your paintings. While in Switzerland Dietrich gets full credit for his work, he is nonetheless often perceived as the Rousseau from Switzerland. That seems to lead to why this will be such a perfect match to show your work and Dietrich's work together, because your praxis is very much working from these misunderstandings in visual culture—and there is a great potential in productive misunderstandings.

RICHARD PHILLIPS:
I'm often referred to as a hyperrealist or Pop artist. The deliberate use of stylistic as well as visual misinformation in my work is, in the way that it interrupts the possibility of establishing correct narratives, something that I deliberately do. Putting them in context with Dietrich as an inspiration speaks to this condition of misrepresentation and misreading.
And that's a deliberate way to reframe or recontextualize aspects of my work. In a way, it undoes a kind of critical distance and opens up vulnerability in my own process.

BEATRIX RUF:
Being too "Pop" in the sense of *not* having critical distance.

RICHARD PHILLIPS:
In combining my work with Dietrich's, I am exploring the ways in which art gets used and misused, and to what degree intentionality plays a part in that. Let's take the example of my painting Message Force Multiplier. The title refers to the New York Times term for when a general is speaking as an expert on a news program, say Fox television, in order to give his expert opinion on how the war is going along in Iraq, but is, at the same time, actually working as a lobbyist for the military-industrial complex, selling weaponry to the same government whose war he's commenting on. Within the context of my shows, paintings can appear to be communicating in one way, while in combinations with other works have a completely conflicting agenda of representation, just as a message force multiplier would. A message force multiplier becomes an active switching point in its perpetuation of falsehoods, in its relation to beauty and death. By exhuming its own beauty, this falsehood lives again to resell itself to a new, targeted demographic.

BEATRIX RUF:
Can you talk about the particular choice of paintings by Dietrich you're using? You seem to have been particularly attracted to the intense and dark winter sea-landscapes, which transport a lot the historical context and difficulties of the times they were painted—but for your full appropriations, you choose totally different ones.

RICHARD PHILLIPS:
Libertas [2010] has in its background a landscape with storm clouds coming over Lake Constance. The consequences of this type of meteorological formation are serious, and in Dietrich's personal history these foreboding landscapes serve as a metaphor for his anxiety over the rise of the war across the lake in Germany. In Libertas, I appropriate the portrait of a former propaganda agent for the Nazis, Libertas Schulze-Boysen, which was taken by the SS immediately before her execution for being a double agent in the Berlin resistance. So it is an image of actual heroism, of actual commitment, of literally having one's life terminated by a malevolent entity because of one's commitment to ideals that were against this reigning power structure. Libertas knew that her death was imminent, but at the same time, she knew what she had accomplished in terms of her activities with the resistance in Berlin. So there is a dual psychological weight that was intended to be paired with that specific landscape and to show that histories are running parallel to each other in order to amplify what insurgency and true resistance are. Then, on another extreme, there are the cat paintings both Dietrich and I made. Of course, Dietrich was never afraid of getting into seriously quaint and intimate painting. He made several paintings of baskets of kittens. The one that I wanted to show was Persia [1996], which is a portrait of a cat that I got from a pet store when I was buying food for a friend's cat. That single painting can on one hand address complex psychological representations and on the other render the tenderest images of universal sentiment, reflecting painting's potential to create a deliberate collision of languages in order to ruin the logic of intentionality. The idea of Dietrich making paintings that, on a metaphorical level, spoke to the conditions that people were living in directly before the war represents something beyond the need to represent an environment. There was a palpable sense of alienation and an inhuman quality in those paintings. To place one of my appropriated images in that context was to literally bring those two elements together and make them inseparable, to point to the romantic

potential of narrative. For me, those relationships are very specific: the impending doom of the sky in that painting reflects what the consequences of her actions were; the emptiness and the depopulated beauty of <u>Message Force Multiplier</u> was the coefficient for the marine's emptiness as a model of a type of attraction that was being put in every teenager's magazine across this country. I combined those forces to speak about the use of beauty and narrative for negative purposes.

BEATRIX RUF:
That seems very much also to relate to this previously stated dual fascination, with how on one hand painting has been critically discussed in production, but on the other hand you have the still life, the full appropriations. Also, critical distance in your practice often seems to be created in groups of images you combine, things together as thoughts together. This readability of the critical, even political, content is revealed if you see a combination of your work being brought in relationship. It occurred to me that this is also working in the painting exhibition you put together with David Salle.

RICHARD PHILLIPS:
There are painters in that show who believe in the veracity of the medium, and then there are those who acknowledge it as false and use it anyway to perpetuate the sense that painting is an act of managing falsehoods. Within that show, the use of photography and of graphic design by some of the artists is important in the way in which it shows the difference between the believers and the non-believers. I believe in the potential of painting as a communicative device with all of its negative attributes fully intact, with the criticism assigned; there is texture and quality in that very criticism. Painting—particularly issues of aesthetics within it—can have an insurgent conceptual potential, but the realization of that potential is not something that's going to happen overtly; that is, by nature, the concept can remain buried in the work, and then depending on the context can explode its meaning right in the face of individuals. To me, one of the important parts of that exhibition was that the combination of works showed revealed that possibility.

BEATRIX RUF:
So the Richard Phillips/Adolf Dietrich show is an interesting complication of what believing and non-believing means.

RICHARD PHILLIPS:
Yes, actually, it can be. The use of painting, for me, has the capacity to slow things down, and to manipulate time in a certain sense to be able to gain access to that type of discussion, or at least to open up that type of discussion. It creates a potential, for me at least. I say, why not be able to use the specialized nature of a form to bring people into it? That's where the seduction is used in propaganda or in media, so why as an artist wouldn't I choose to do that?

BEATRIX RUF:
Two believers, then?

RICHARD PHILLIPS:
I think the danger is that one assumes that Dietrich was trying to do that too, and that's why I'm interested in him as an artist. It's not. Actually, it's the very fact that he wasn't; that he was absolutely free from that, that he worked on his art apart from the constrictions of a linearly determined modernist interpretation. I think that I'm trying to do the same thing but from a different direction—I'm trying to deal with the obviously changed, but in some cases parallel, conditions that we live in today. There is no mistaking why the marine was set against the Dietrich's frozen world, or why Libertas Schulze-Boysen was set against the image of Dietrich's stormy landscape. Those were chosen relationships—because of the doubling of agency, melded with the doubling of experience, the repeating of history.

BEATRIX RUF:
What are the most exciting things that can happen in this show?

RICHARD PHILLIPS:
The experience of being physically in front of these paintings and seeing how they in fact do communicate, my paintings and his paintings. I think that this show will look into painting as a form of communi-cation—not only what its limitations are, but actually what its power is and what its capacities are to communicate, and its potential for being used and misused from a number of different directions.

BEATRIX RUF:
So many discussions about productive misreading are possible . . .

RICHARD PHILLIPS:
In my own production, since I don't do versions per se, any one of those works could be good enough for a solo show, or could have been seen as a marker in other kinds of conceptual arguments. But the fact that they are made for these constructions—for these stages, since, literally, the show becomes a stage— is not something that's usually attributed to painting, or to the thought process or motivations for making painting at all, in contemporary art. And for me, I think that by pairing that type of production with Dietrich's production, there may be a possibility for interesting parallel assessments of what a form can do, and how it can communicate.

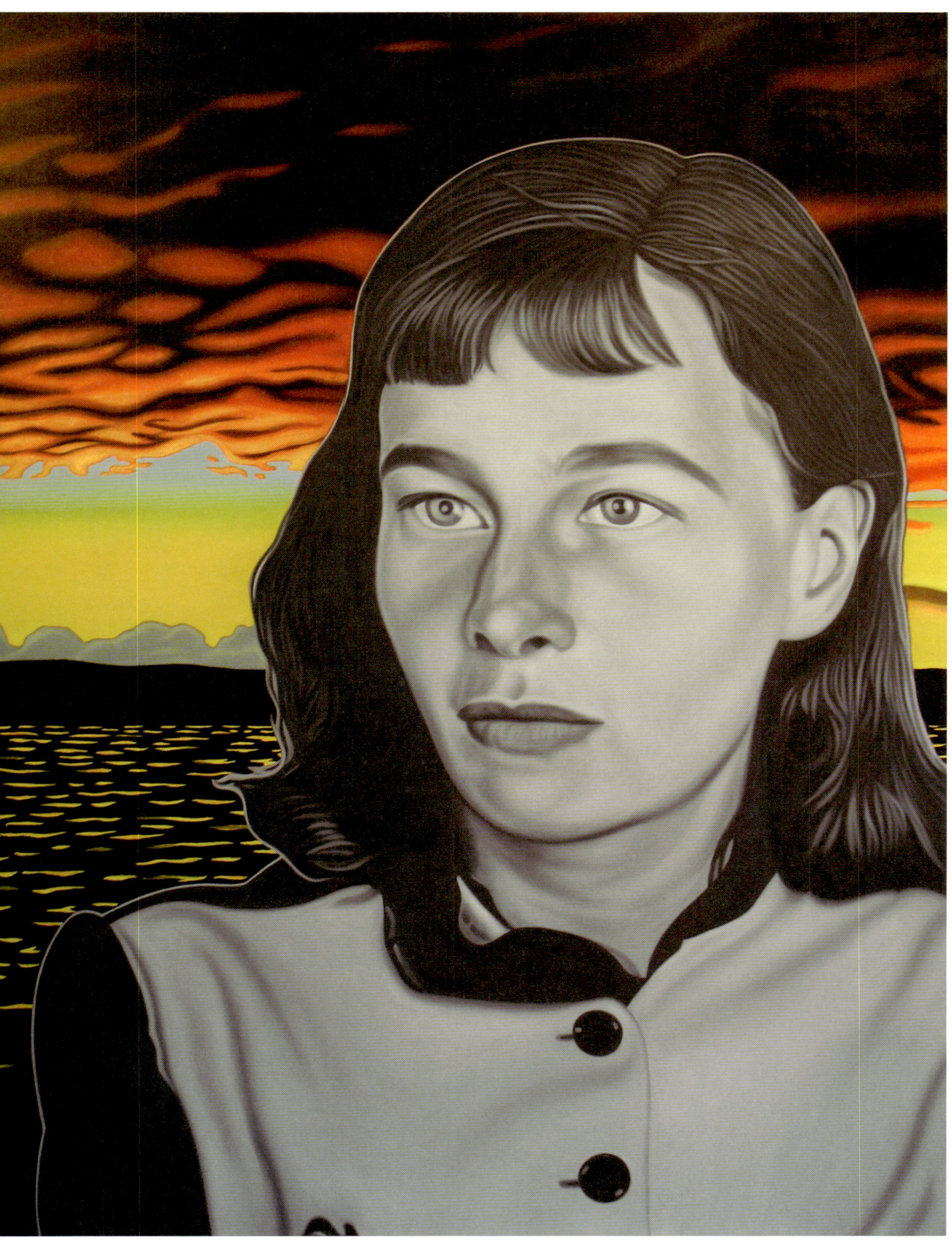

Left–right:
Richard Phillips
Libertas
2010
102 x 79.3 in. / 229.1 x 201.4 cm
Oil on linen
Courtesy of the artist and
Gagosian Gallery, New York

Adolf Dietrich
Rote Abendwolken über dem See
1917
15.2 x 19.1 in. / 38.5 x 48.5 cm
Oil on cardboard
Kunstmuseum Winterthur

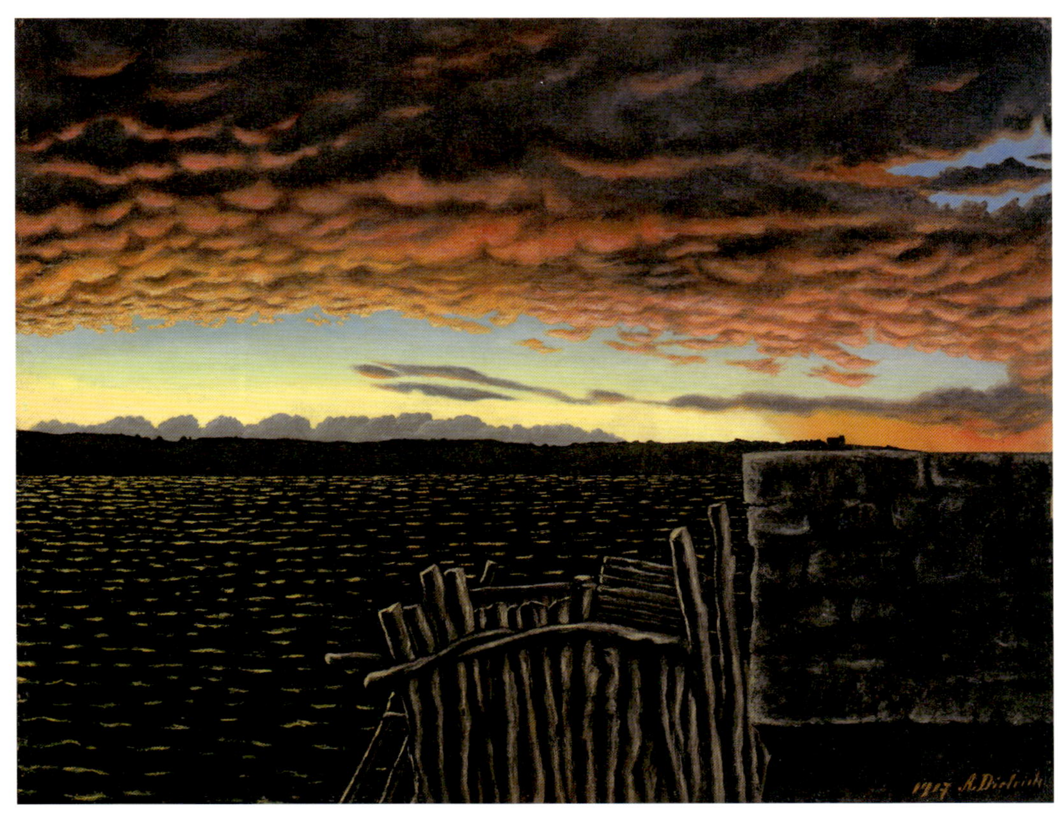

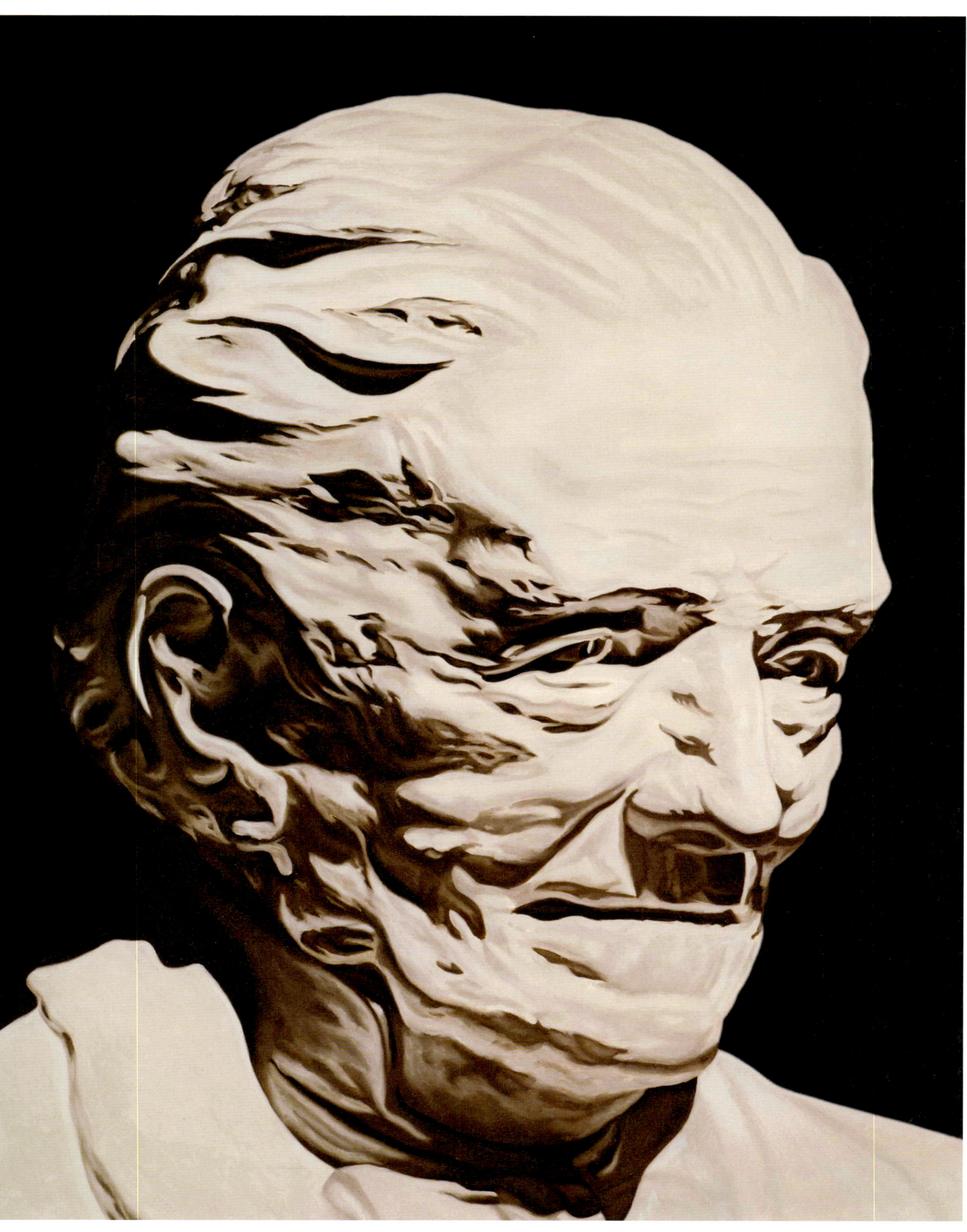

Left–right:
Richard Phillips
Old Granddad
2001
84 x 65.5 in. / 213.4 x 166.6 cm
Oil on canvas
Private collection

Adolf Dietrich
Vater, die Zeitung lesend
1913
24 x 20.1 in. / 61 x 51 cm
Oil on canvas
Kunstmuseum des Kantons Thurgau,
Ittinger Museum

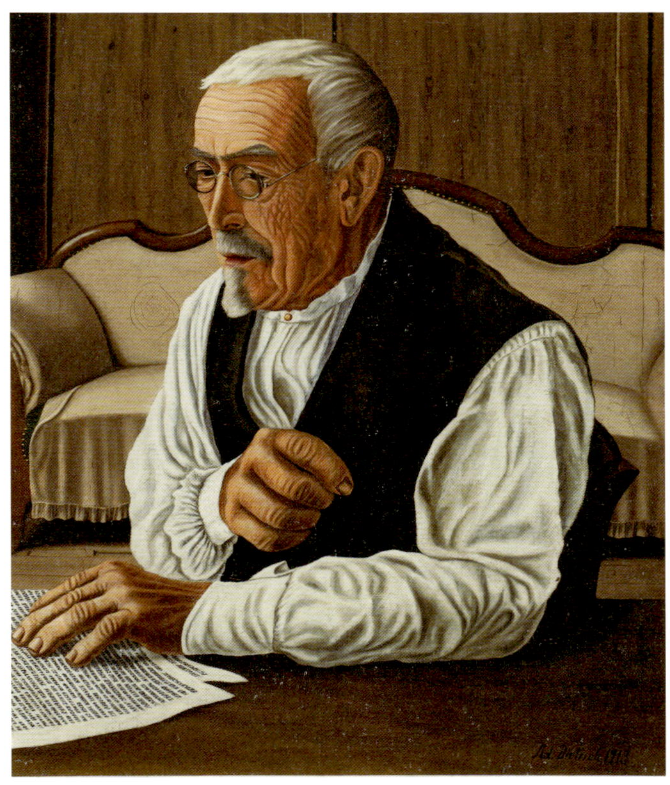

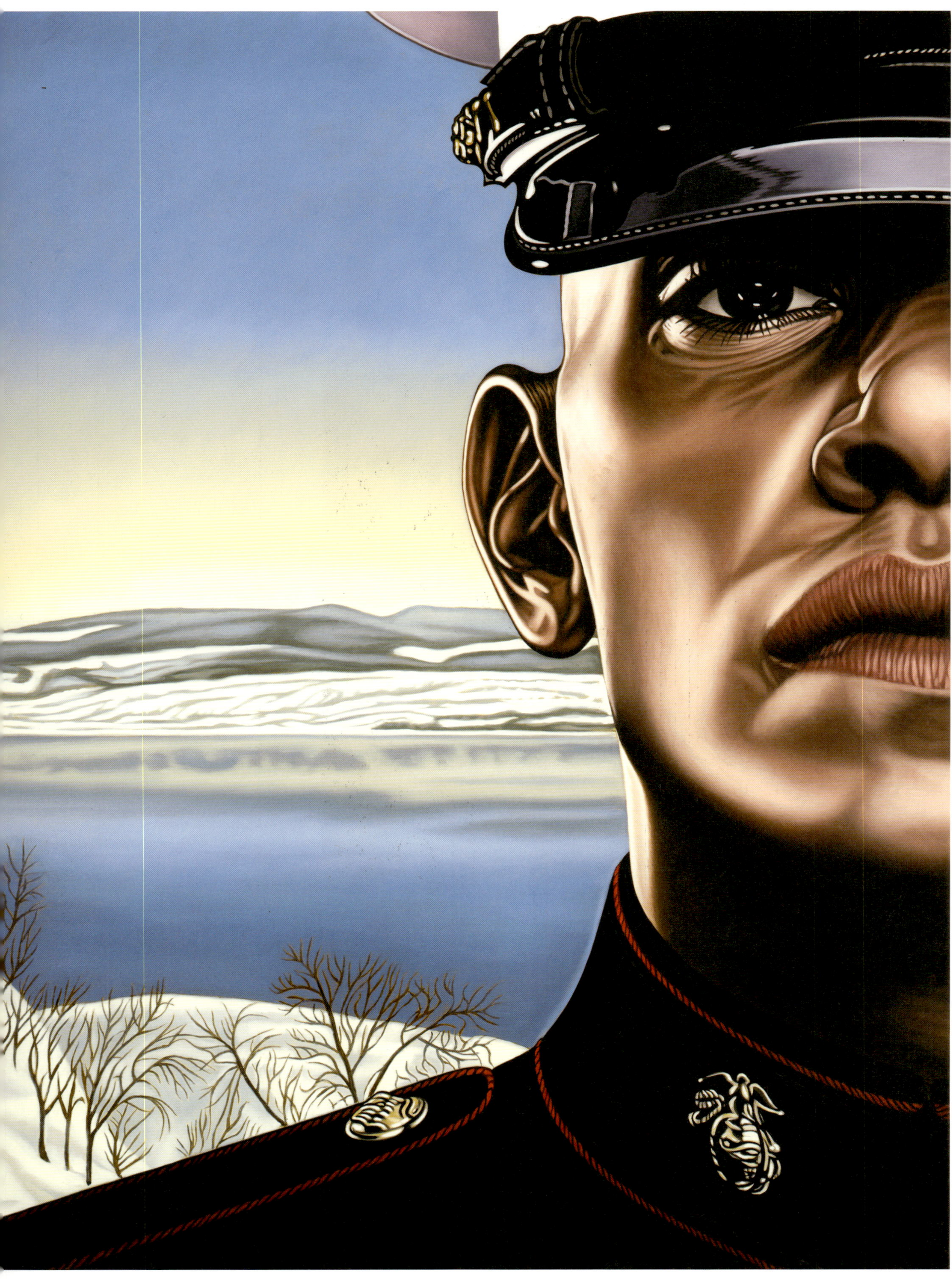

Left–right:
Richard Phillips
Message Force Multiplier
2009
78 x 58.3 in. / 198.1 x 148.1 cm
Oil on linen
Pinnell Collection

Adolf Dietrich
Winter am Untersee
1941
18.1 x 23.4 in. / 46 x 59.5 cm
Oil on cardboard
Kunsthaus Zurich

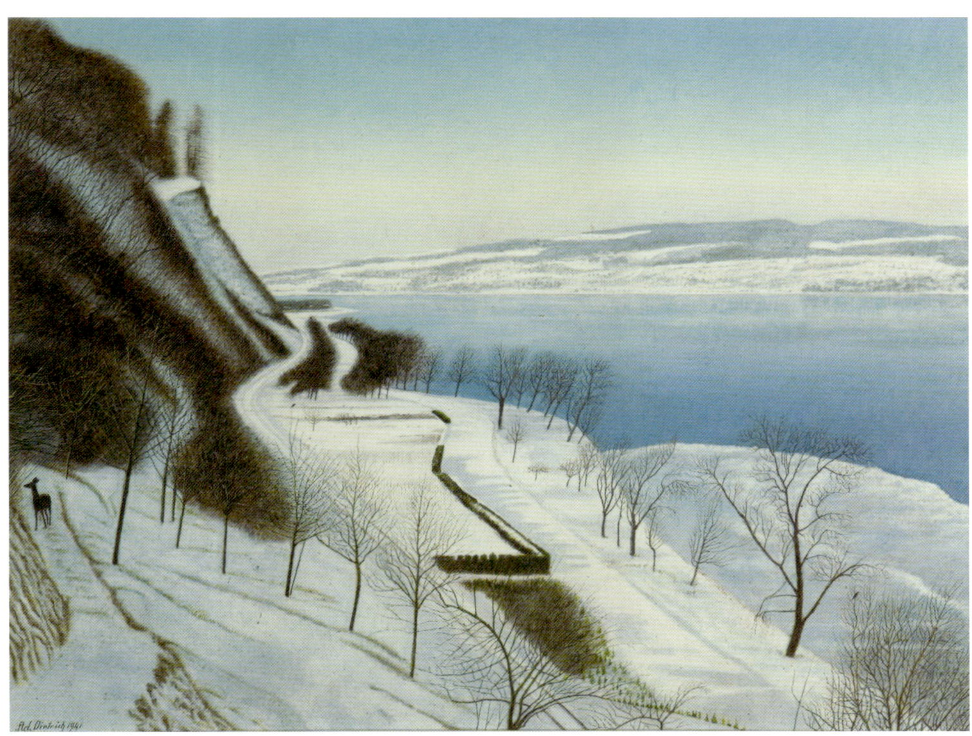

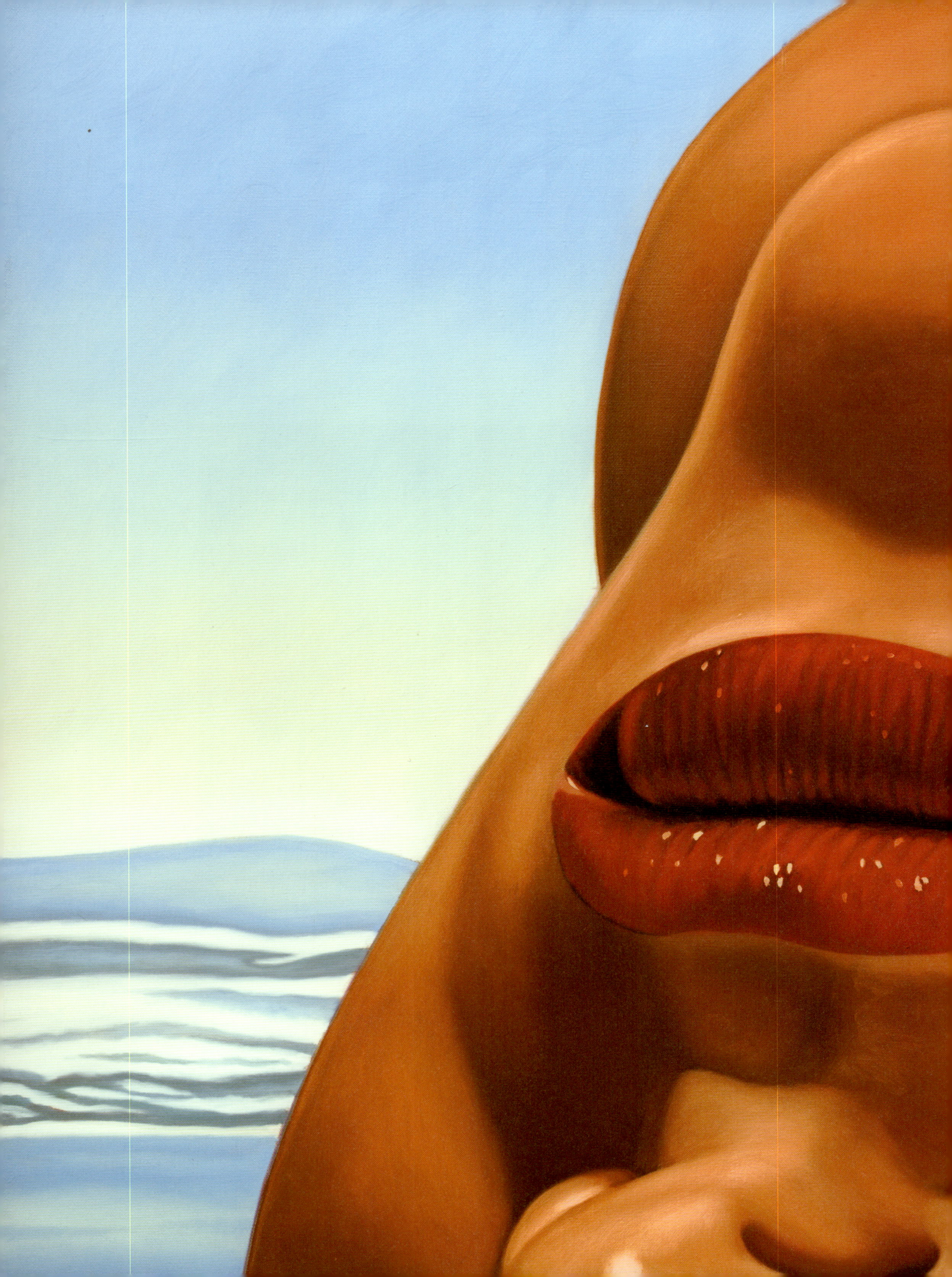

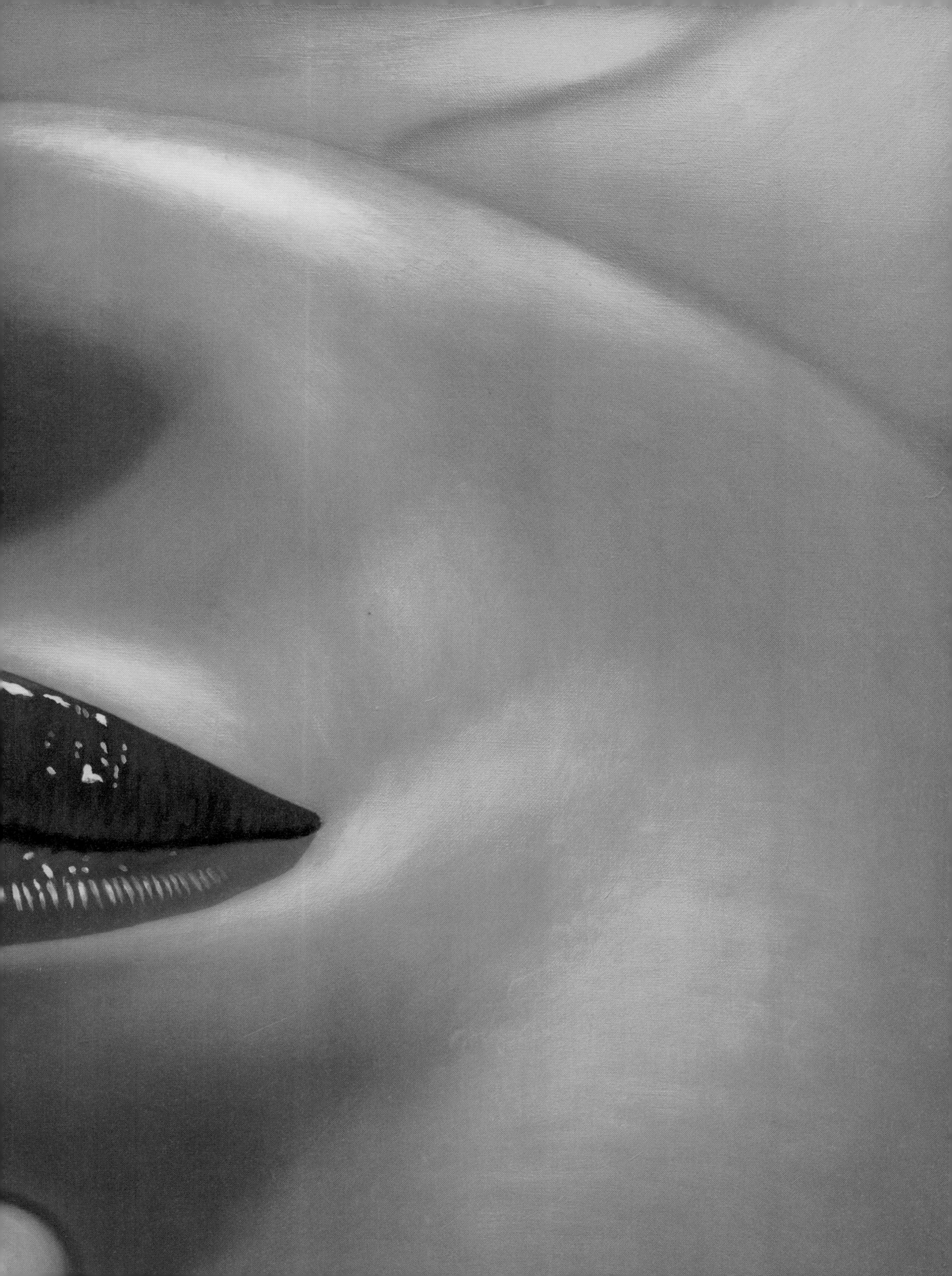

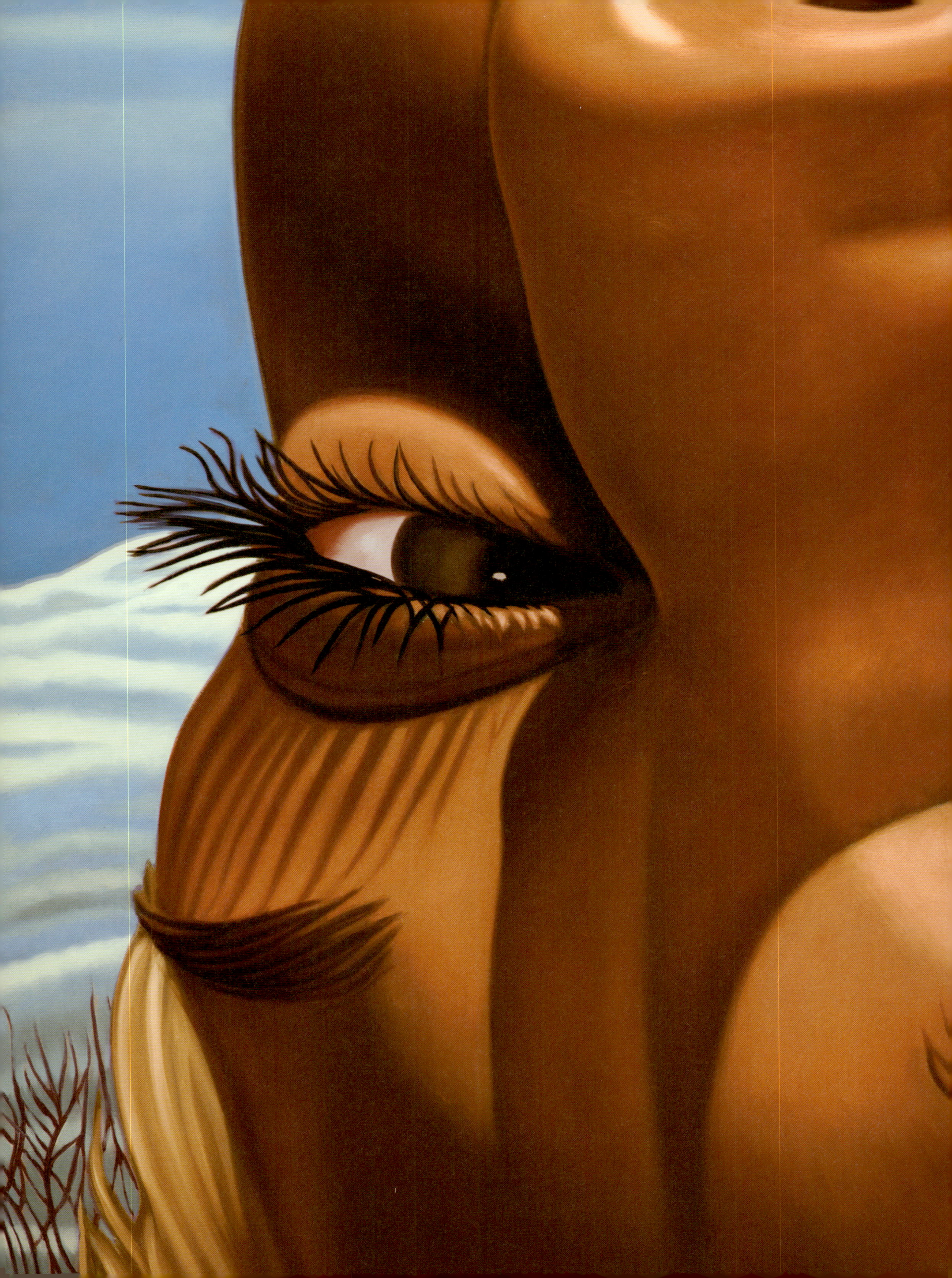

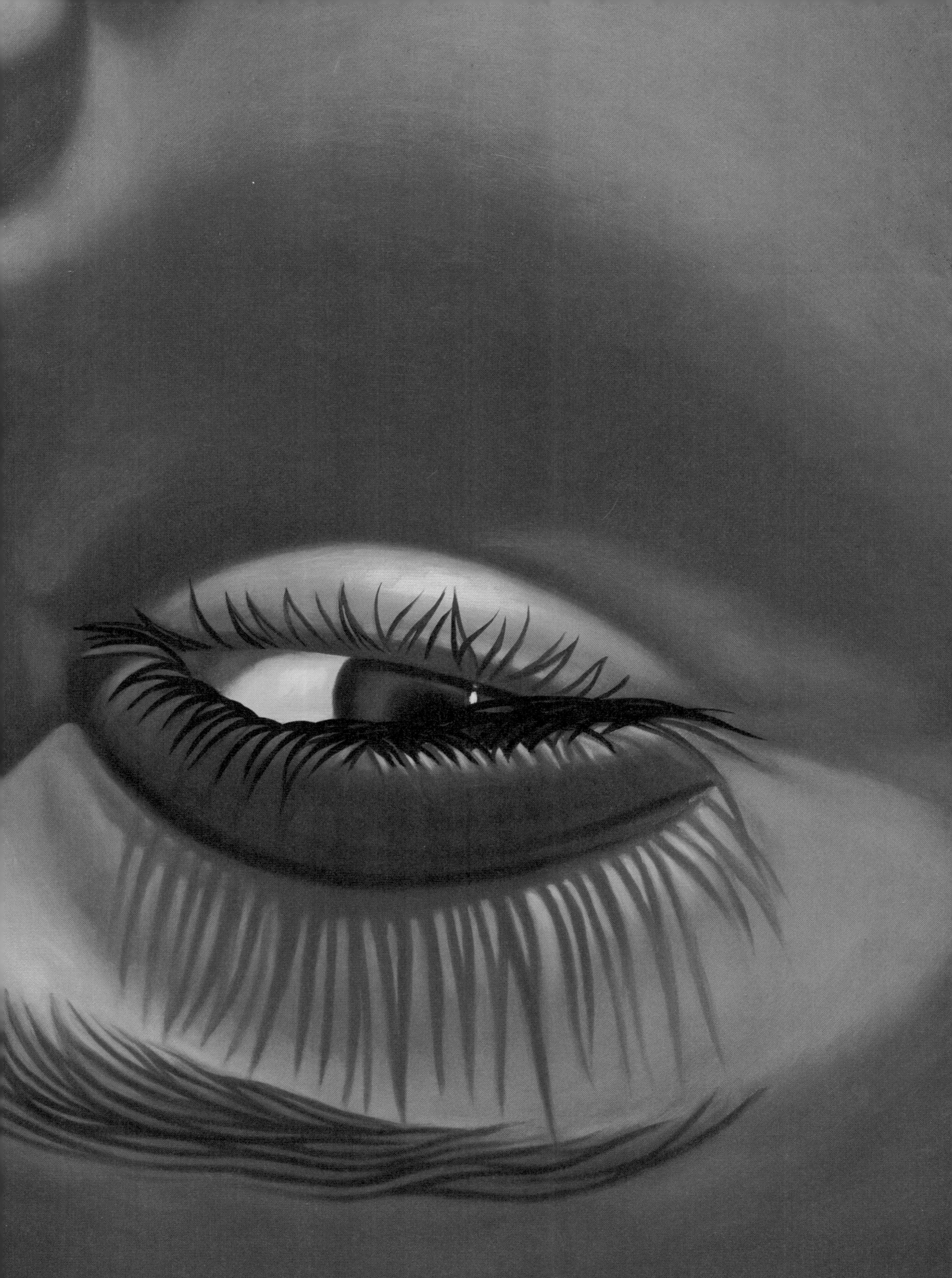

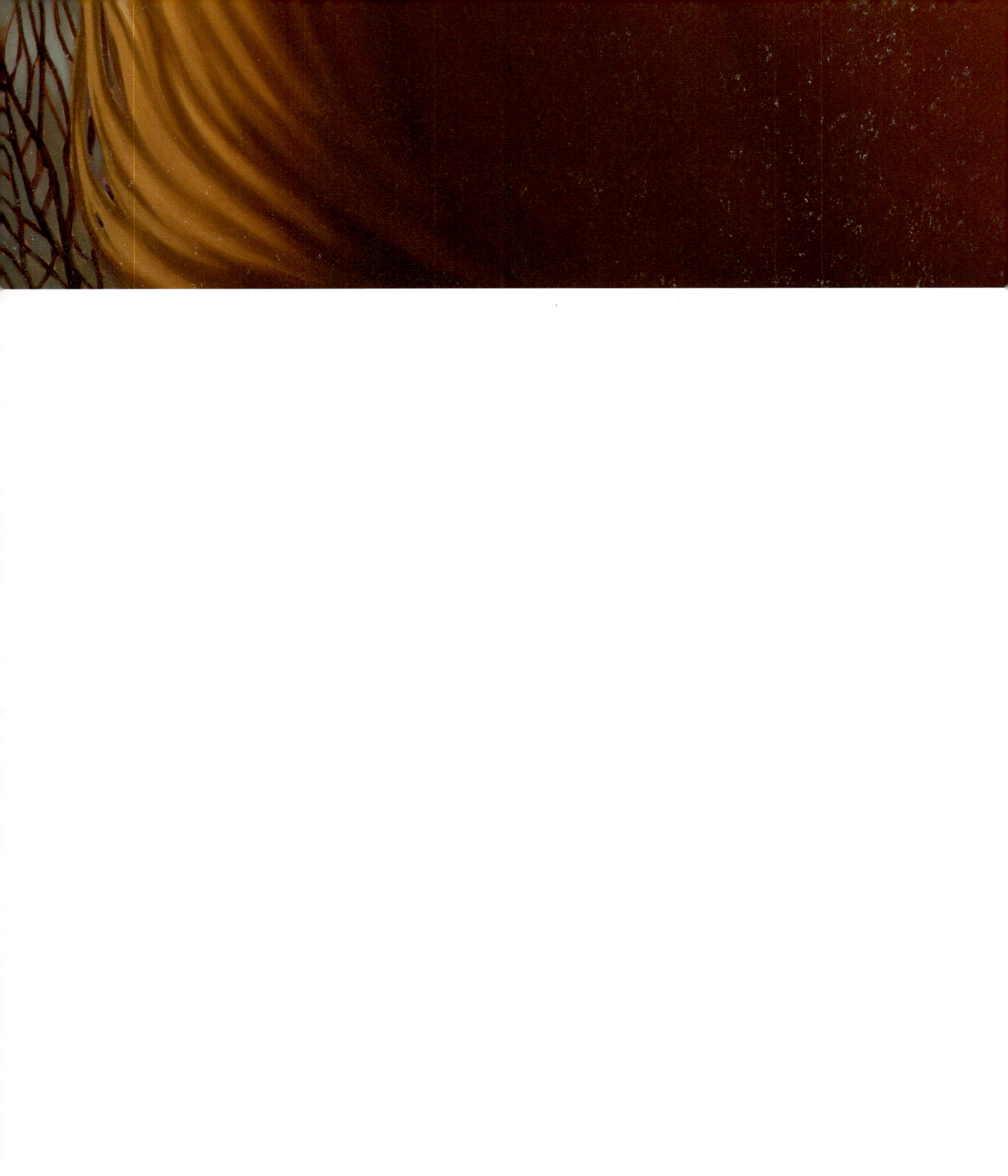

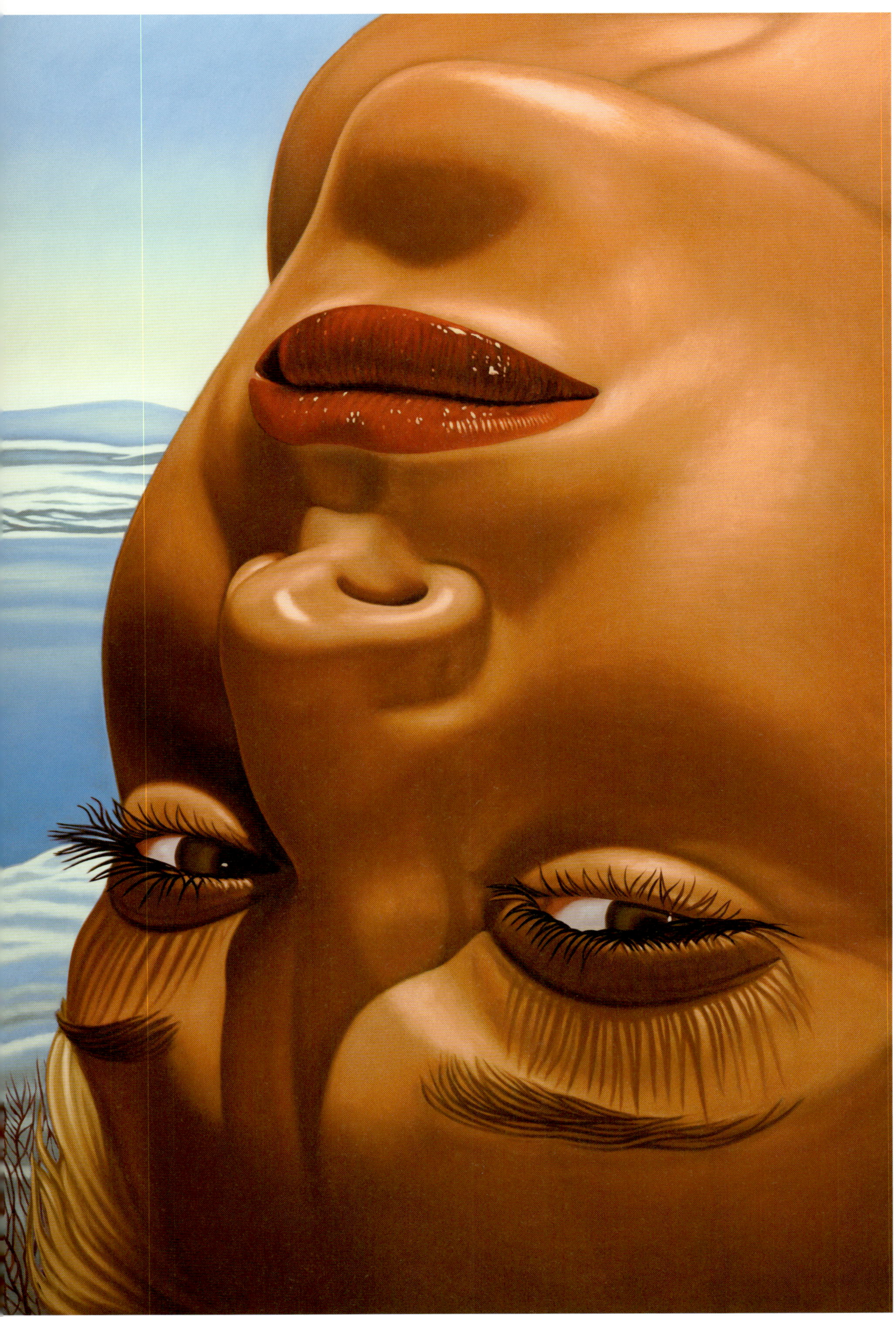

1/6-6/6 and Left–right:
Richard Phillips
<u>Der Bodensee</u>
2008
78 x 52.5 in. / 198.1 x 133.4 cm
Oil on linen
Private collection

Adolf Dietrich
<u>Winter am Untersee</u>
1941
18.1 x 23.4 in. / 46 x 59.5 cm
Oil on cardboard
Kunsthaus Zurich

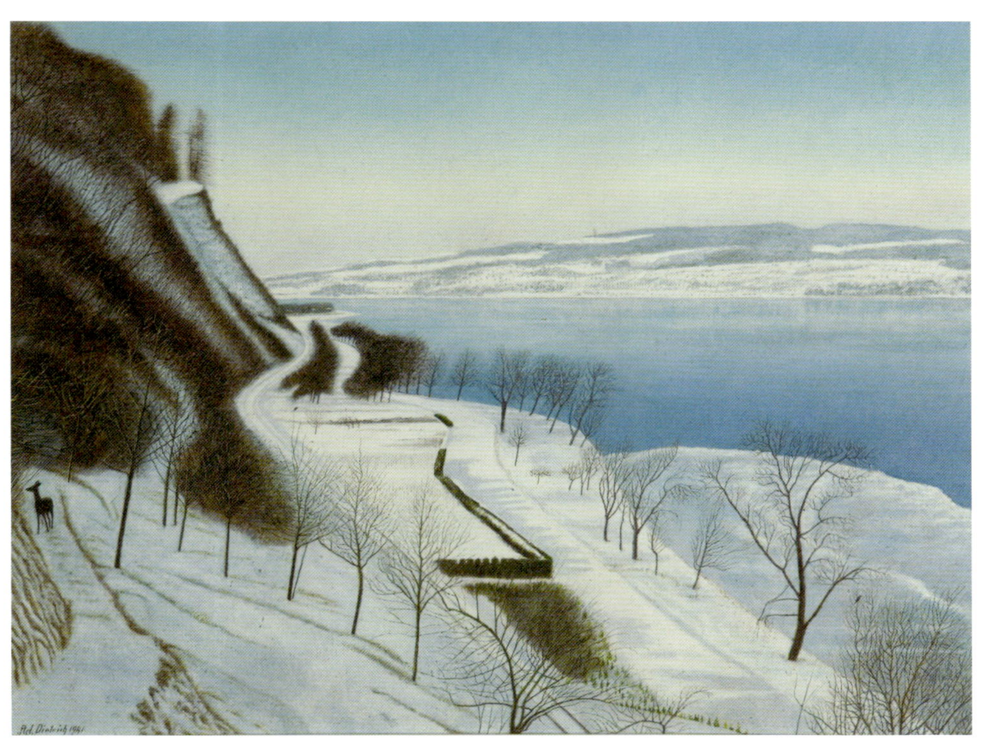

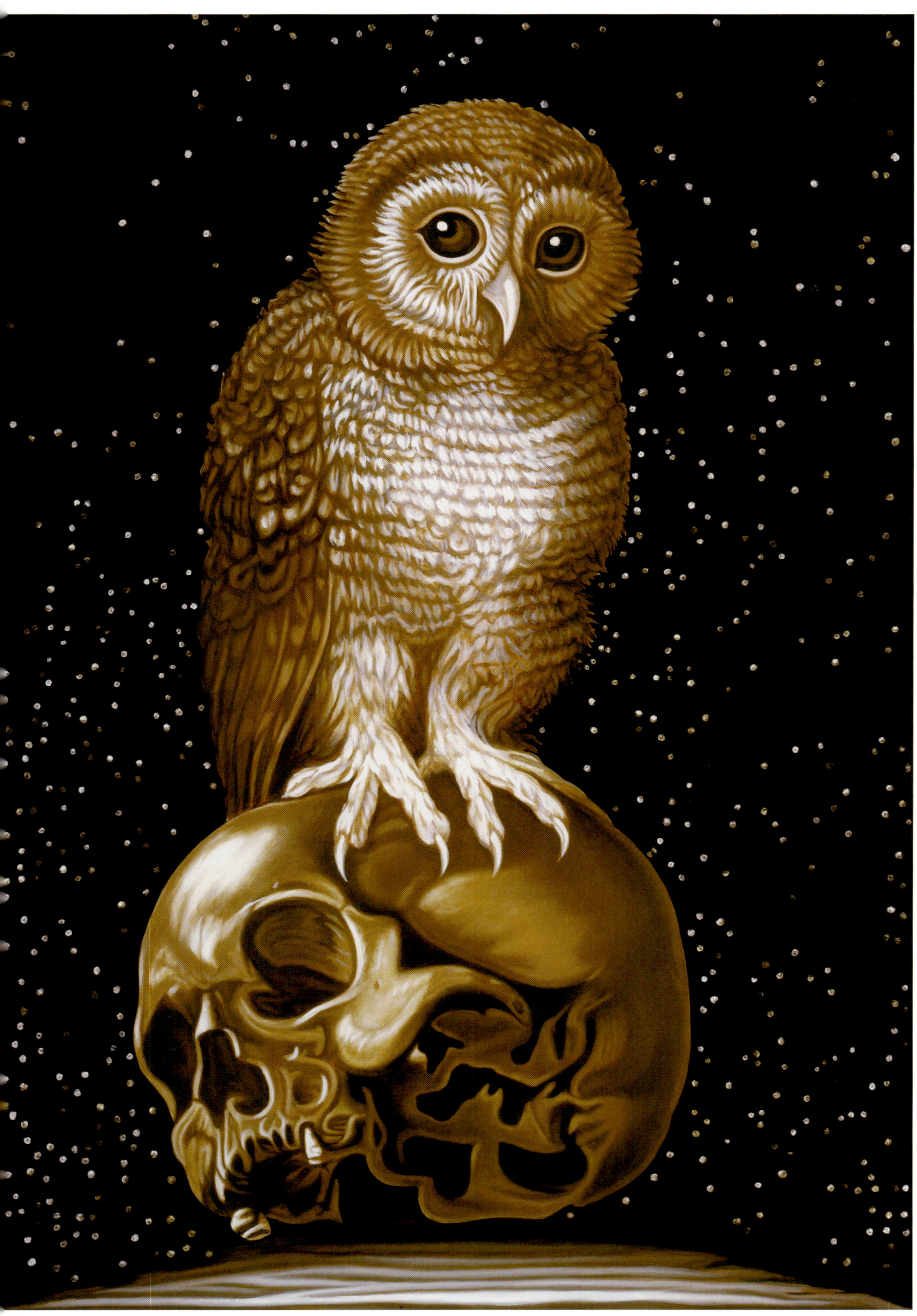

Left–right:
Richard Phillips
Vanitas
2007
108 x 74 in. / 274.3 x 188 cm
Oil on linen
Private collection

Adolf Dietrich
Waldkäuze im Tobel
1929
33.1 x 23.2 in. / 84 x 59 cm
Oil on cardboard
Private collection

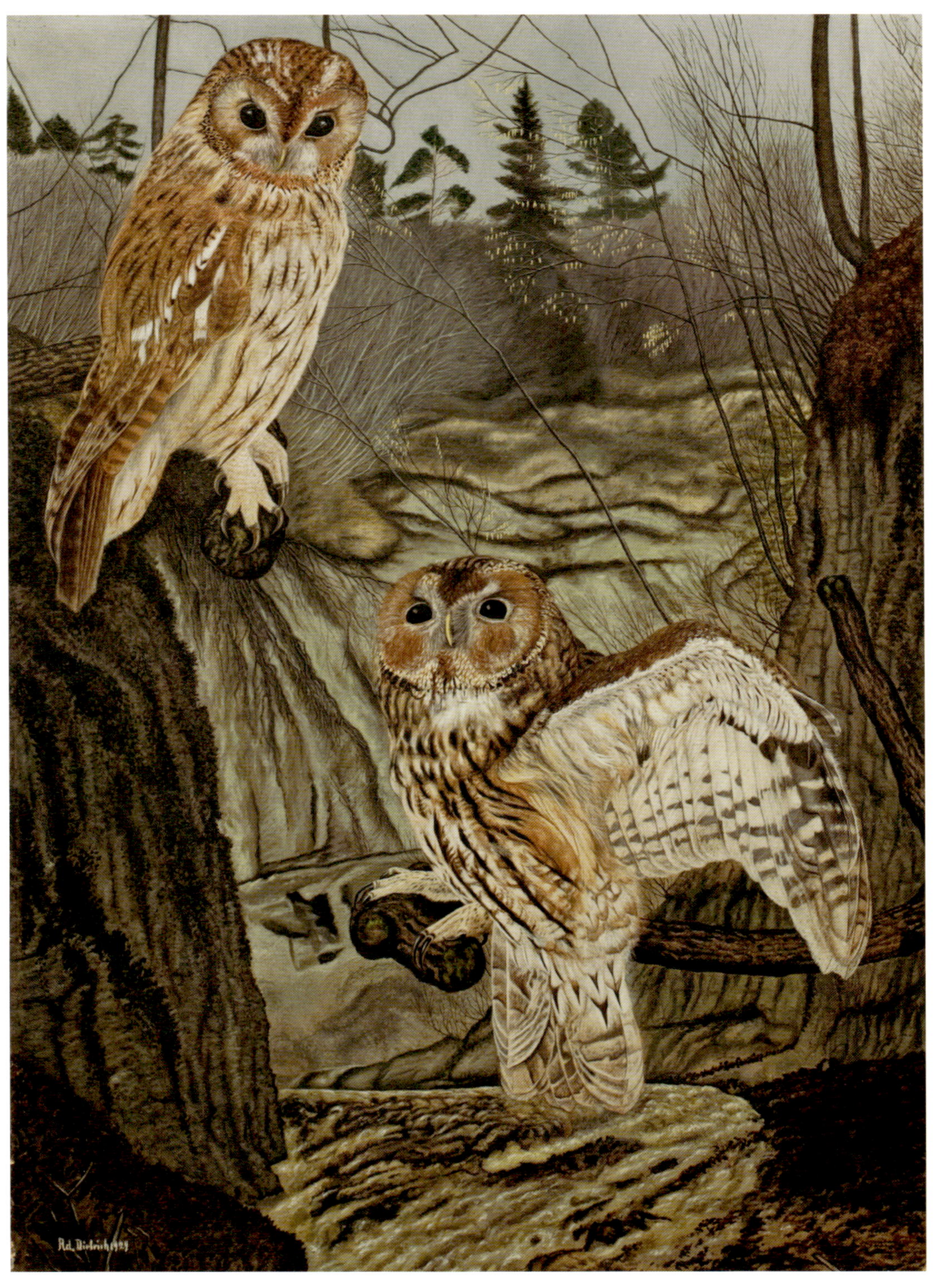

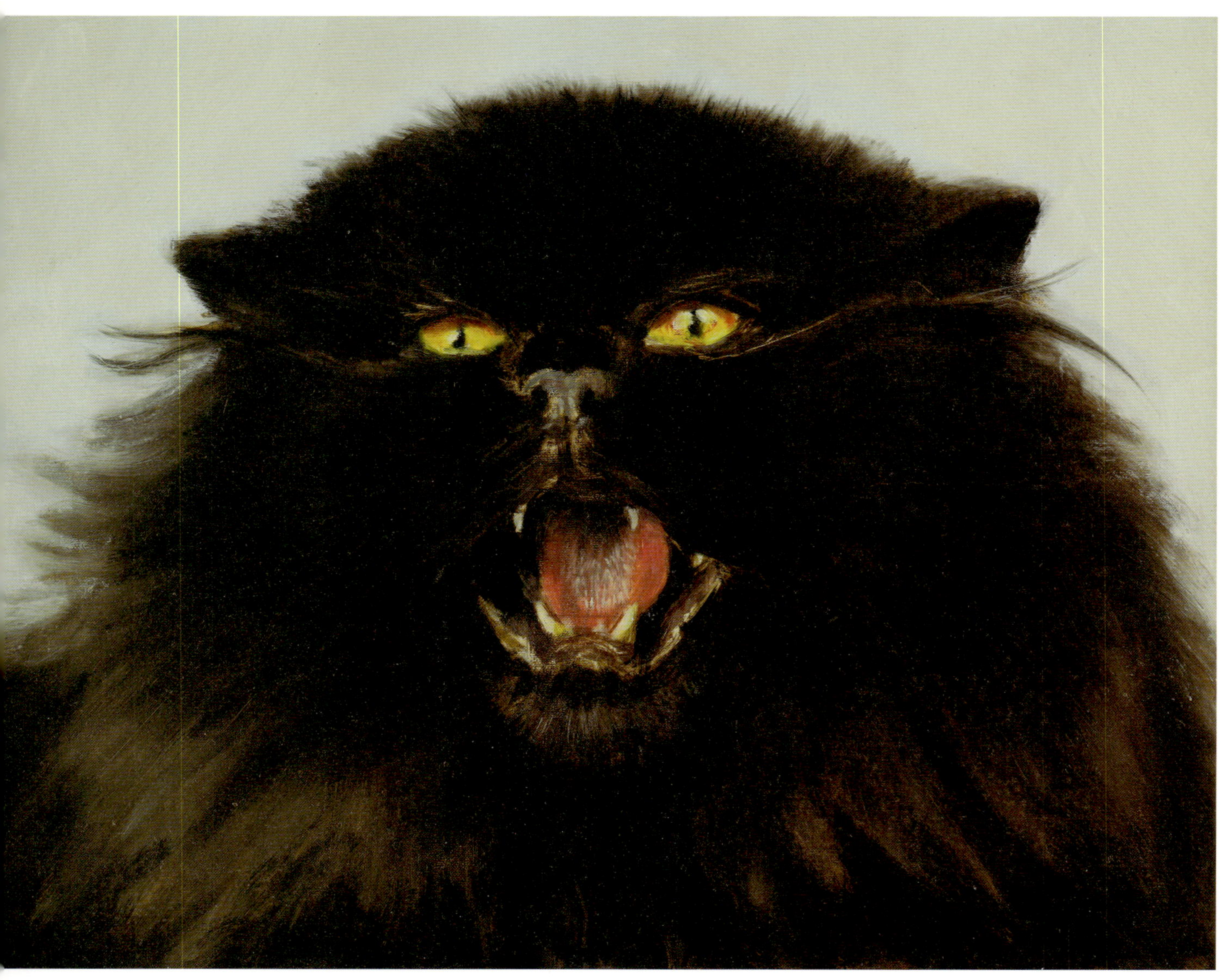

Left–right:
Richard Phillips
Mouser
1997
16 x 20 in. / 40.6 x 50.8 cm
Oil on linen
Private collection

Adolf Dietrich
Zwei Angorakätzchen
1925
14.4 x 13.6 in. / 36.5 x 34.5 cm
Oil on cardboard
Private collection

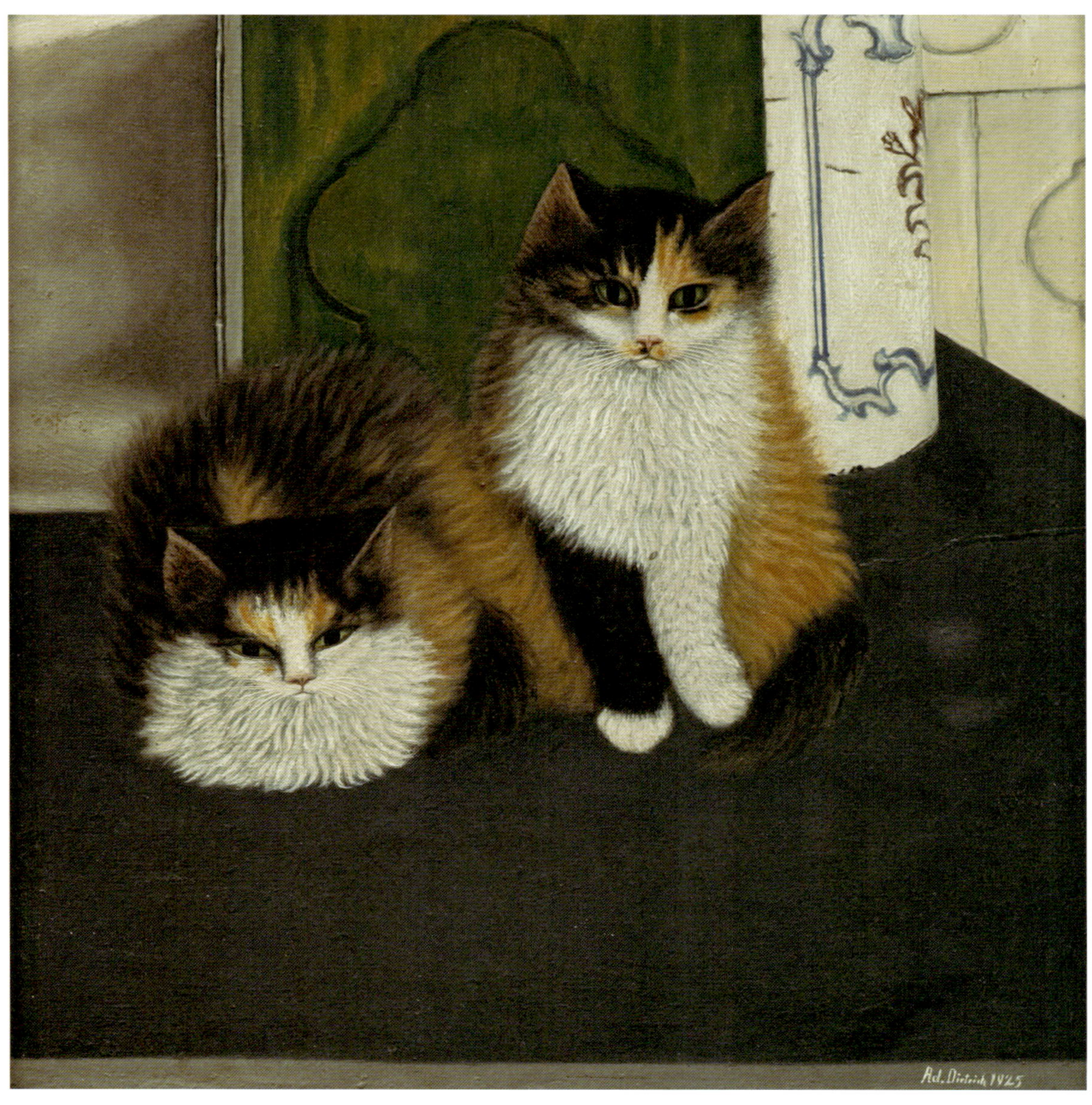

Adolf Dietrich
Zaine mit jungen Kätzchen
1934
16.5 x 19.9 in. / 42 x 50.5 cm
Oil on plywood
Private collection

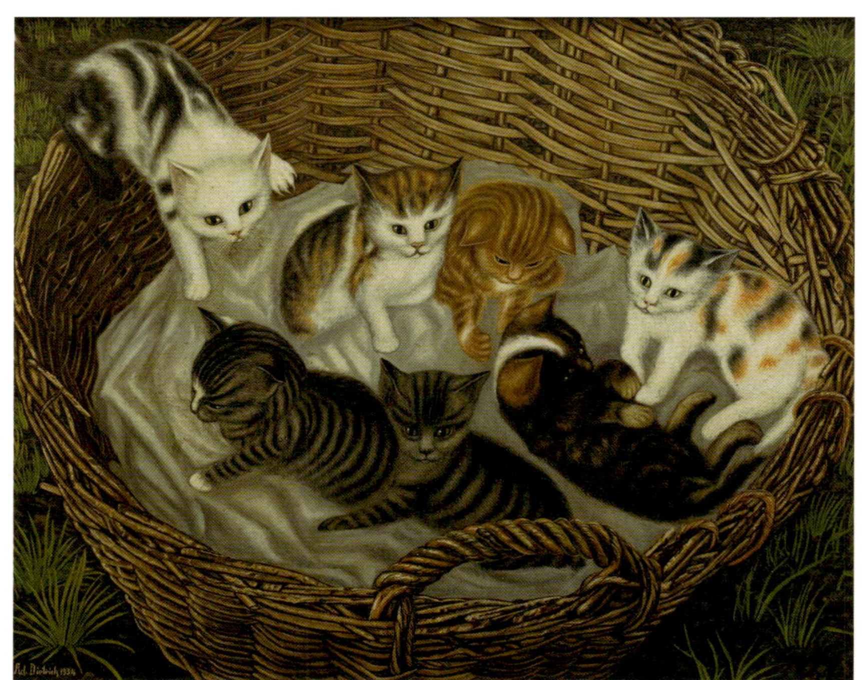

Adolf Dietrich
Drei tote Marder
1942
29.9 x 19.9 in. / 76 x 50.5 cm
Oil on wood
Private collection

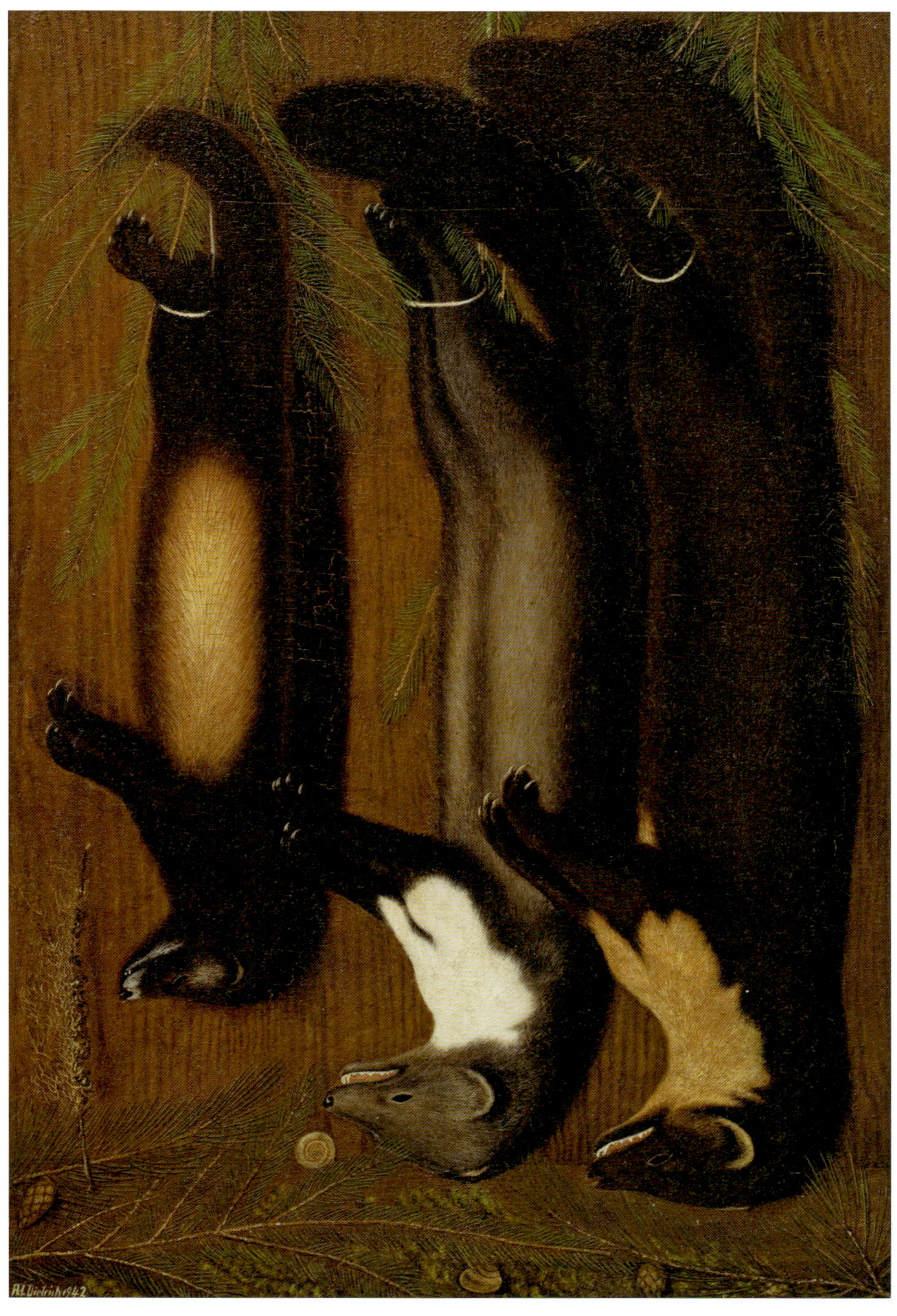

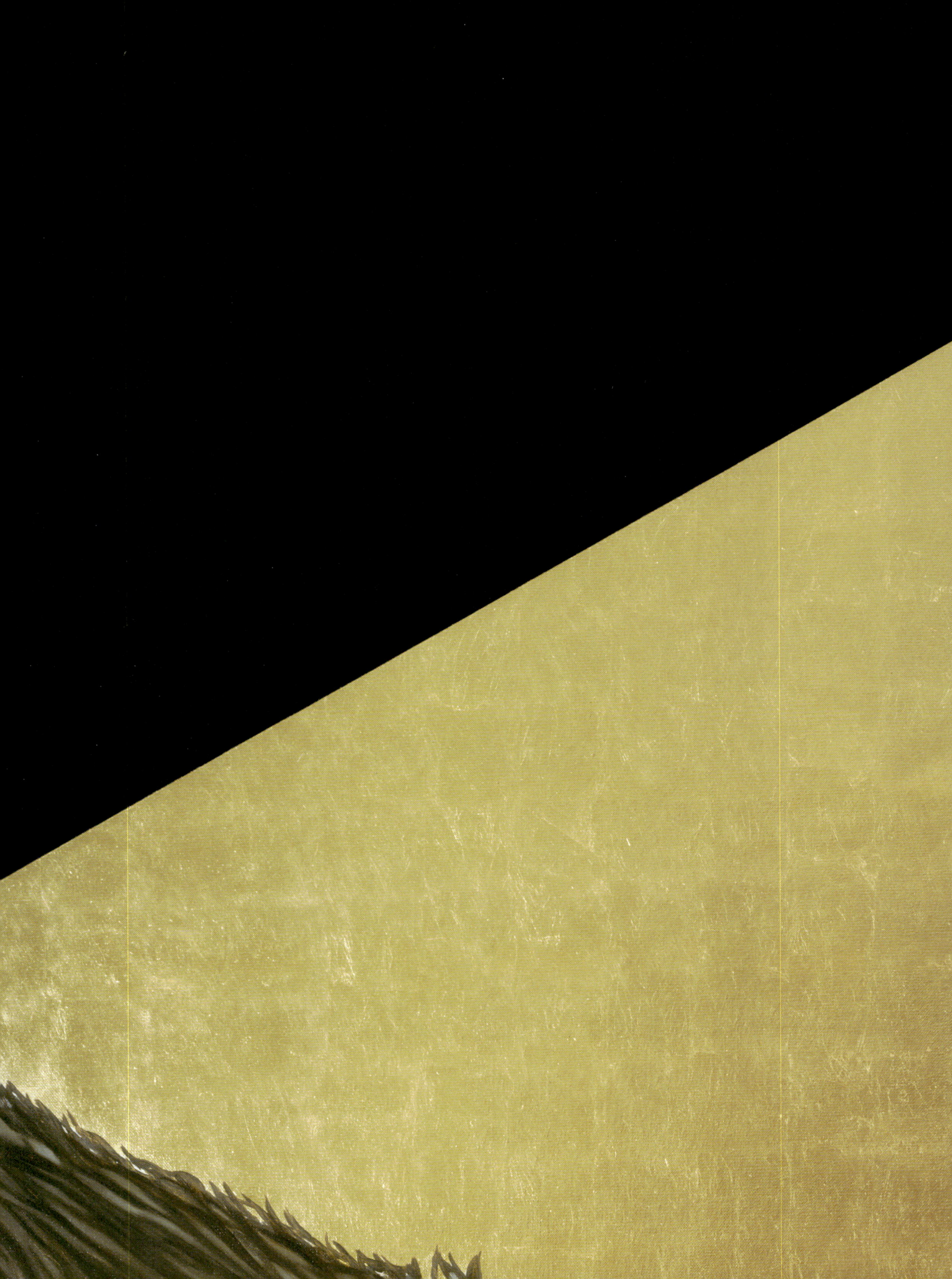

1/4:
Richard Phillips
Were You of Silver,
Were You of Gold?
2009
82 x 60 in. / 208.3 x 152.4 cm
Oil on linen
Courtesy of the artist and
Gagosian Gallery, New York

THE DIETRICH ENIGMA

BY DOROTHEE MESSMER

TRANSLATION BY SUSAN BERNOFSKY

There are no end of stories and suppositions about Adolf Dietrich—his life offered ample material for projections and continues to do so. The biography of this textile mill worker and day laborer who became a celebrated artist suggests fairy-tale-like parallels to *Cinderella* or the *Brave Little Tailor*, associations that tap into our longing for stories, especially those with punch lines. And there is no shortage of these in Dietrich's life, as witnessed by the memories large and small described in all the first, second and third-hand accounts currently in circulation.

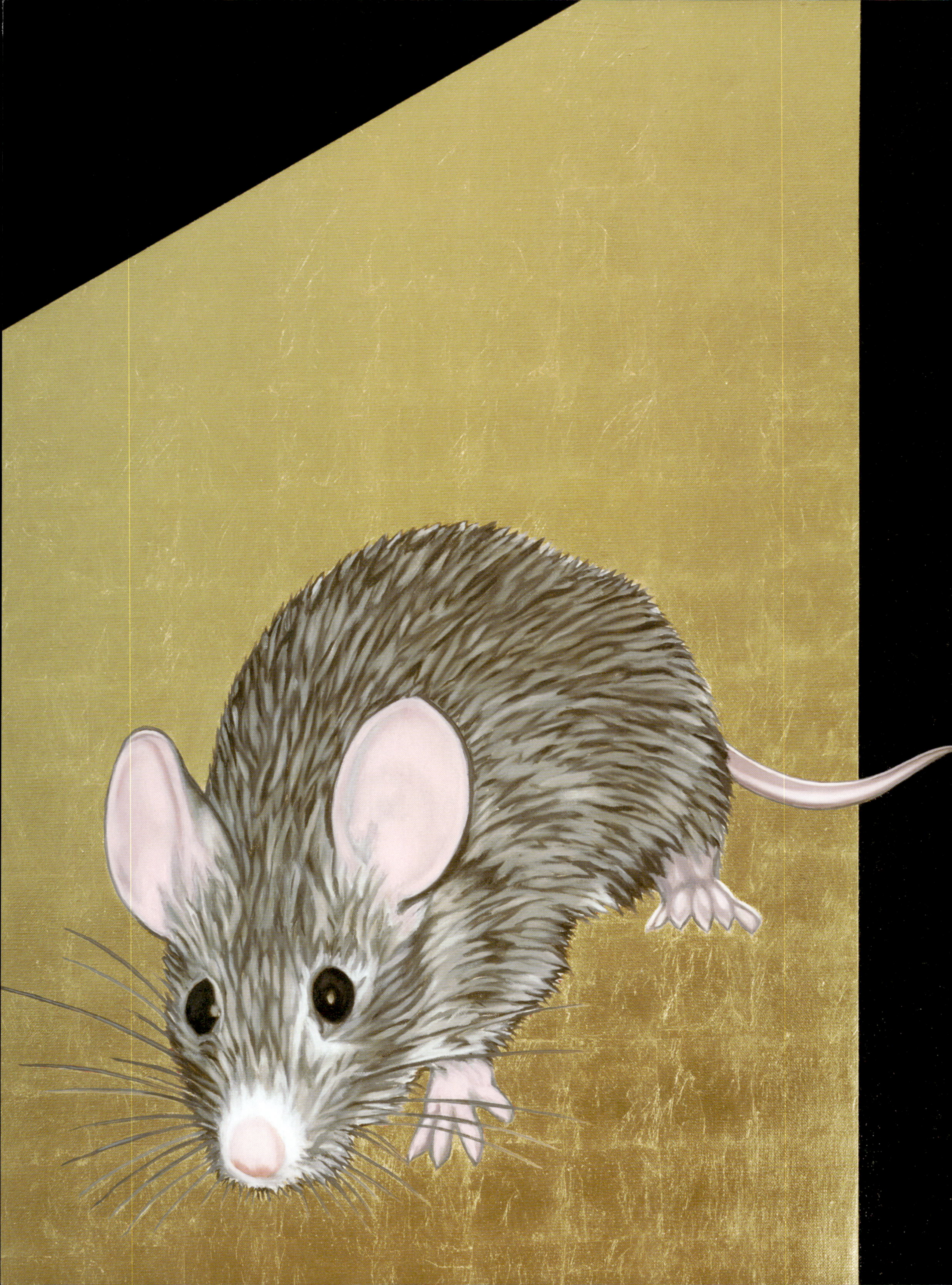

2/4:
Richard Phillips
<u>Were You of Silver,</u>
<u>Were You of Gold?</u>
2009
82 x 60 in. / 208.3 x 152.4 cm
Oil on linen
Courtesy of the artist and
Gagosian Gallery, New York

1. Adolf Dietrich in a letter to
Willi F. Storck, Kunsthalle Mannheim
(Jan 15, 1919), in: Adolf Dietrich.
Malermeister–Meistermaler.
Ein Glossar, Hg. Kunstmuseum
Thurgau, Sulgen / Zürich 2002, p. 16.

2. ibid.

3. Paul Fink in a lettter to Adolf Dietrich
(Nov. 9, 1909), in: *Malermeister–*
Meistermaler, p. 32.

The foundation that all these stories point back to has its basis in the rural poverty of Dietrich's childhood. The youngest of seven children, he was born in 1877 to a smallholder and his wife on the Swiss shore of Lake Constance. As soon as young Adolf started school, it became clear he had a talent for drawing, and the village schoolmaster tutored him in "drawing from nature" in his free time. For financial reasons, however, Dietrich was unable to pursue formal studies of art.

As he himself recalls, "My desire to receive some sort of training in this [drawing] was strong, of course, but financial restraints, two aging parents and a small plot of land and vineyard, where we also kept cows and pigs, prevented me."[1] And so the boy remained with his parents and earned a little extra on the side with factory labor or by taking in work, or else by working as a temporary laborer in the village.

His first drawings (starting in 1896) and pastels and watercolors (starting in 1900) were made on Sundays, when it rained, or in the evenings in the living room of his parents' house where he was to remain for the rest of his life. He got a few pointers from his brother, and an artist in Basel gave him the advice to paint directly from nature rather than according to his imagination. "Aside from this," Dietrich later writes, "I received no guidance worth mentioning."[2]

In 1909 his pictures were rejected by the Kunsthalle Basel and the big art museums in Zurich, Schaffhausen and Winterthur. He received a letter saying: "At the instructions of our Board, I must write to inform you that at the moment it is not possible to exhibit your pictures, as we are fully occupied with other matters."[3] At the beginning, it was other artists who helped him. For example, in 1913 Bruno Goldschmidt put him in touch with the Kunstverein Konstanz [Constance Art Association] which eventually exhibited two of his pictures. After this, the writer Walter Jerven featured Dietrich's drawings in his journal "Das Bodenseebuch" [The Book of Lake Constance] on several occasions. In 1917 Galerie Hans Goltz in Munich showed several of his pictures. His first real breakthrough in Germany, though, came in 1918 with the exhibition "Das badische Land im Bild" [Baden Countryside in Pictures] at the Kunstverein Mannheim [Mannheim Art Association]. One of the curators there, Herbert Tannenbaum, was struck by Dietrich's work and included it in a show at his own gallery, "Das Kunsthaus." In the second exhibition (1925), all but two of the 40 pictures on display were sold. In 1927, Tannenbaum arranged for 60 of Dietrich's pictures to be shown in a gallery in Berlin. The press praised Dietrich as one of the greatest living painters. This was the beginning of a wave of success in Germany that would break off in the mid-1930s with the recession and the rise of National Socialism. Meanwhile Dietrich bought a camera and began taking photographs in 1926 if not before.

ROMANTICISM, NEW OBJECTIVITY, MODERNISM—
DIETRICH'S RECEPTION IN GERMANY

Dietrich's work was presented in various contexts: In 1932, as his letters reveal, he was exhibited together with *Neue Sachlichkeit* [New Objectivity] painters Theo Champion, Hasso von Hugo, Franz Lenk, Alexander Kanoldt, Georg Schrimpf and Franz Radziwill in the "Gruppe der Sieben" [Group of Seven] show in Bochum. In the same year, his work was shown in Ulm in an exhibition of contemporary romantic painting. Paul Cassirer wrote to him that he was planning, together with Galerie Flechtheim, a "comprehensive exhibition" of "the impulses currently at work in contemporary German art." The Kölnische Kunstverein [Cologne Art Association] included him in an exhibition of "modern German art." And again he was invited to participate in an exhibition in Ulm of "linear painting with the exception of sentimental Heimatkunst [homeland painting] in the style of the old masters."

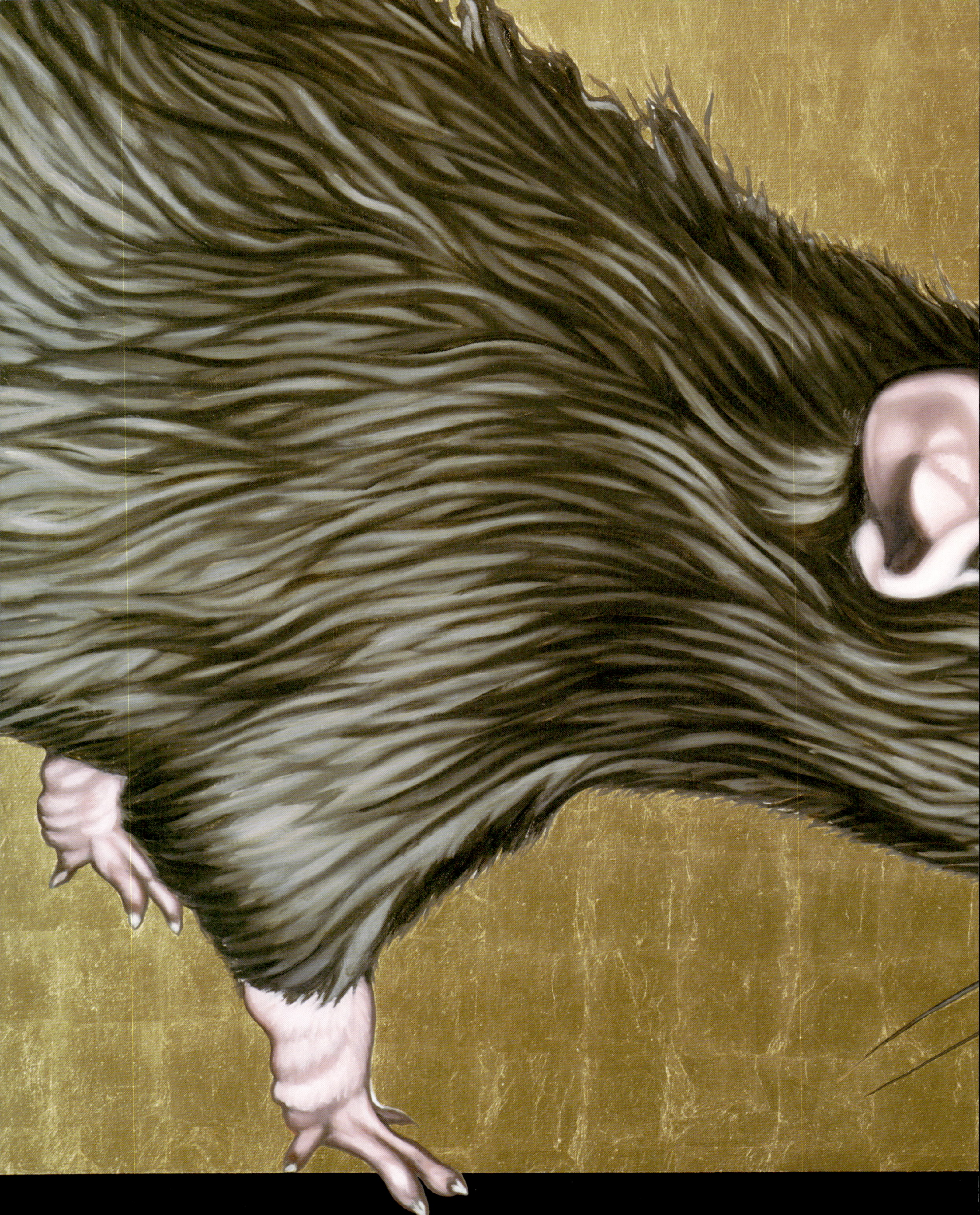

3/4:
Richard Phillips
<u>Were You of Silver,</u>
<u>Were You of Gold?</u>
2009
82 x 60 in. / 208.3 x 152.4 cm
Oil on linen
Courtesy of the artist and
Gagosian Gallery, New York

4. Dr. Hentzen, Nationalgalerie Berlin,
in letter to Adolf Dietrich
(Feb. 1, 1934), in: *Malermeister–
Meistermaler*, p. 44.

The height of Dietrich's success is revealed in his correspondence with the director of the Nationalgalerie in Berlin who wrote to him in 1934: "Now that we have purchased the third picture by you, it is no longer necessary for you to continue to send us paintings […]."[4]

**HOMELAND AND SUNDAY PAINTER, NAÏVE ARTIST—
DIETRICH'S RECEPTION IN SWITZERLAND**

When the invitations from Germany stopped arriving in 1935, Dietrich's image as a naïve painter began to dominate. In 1937 he was included—as the only non-French artist—in the show "Les maitres populaires de la réalité" in Paris. From there the exhibition traveled to London and the United States, where it was shown at the Museum of Modern Art and other American museums.

In Switzerland, interest in Dietrich's work was gradually increasing. The kunstsalon Wolfsberg in Zurich and the Basel gallery owner Bettie Thommen began showing his work regularly starting in the early 1930s. His pictures were exhibited at the Kunstmuseum Winterthur (1926), the Kunstmuseum Schaffhausen (1933) and the Thurgauische Kunstgesellschaft [Thurgau Art Society, 1935].

Dietrich was now beginning to enjoy success in Switzerland as well. The gallery Epoques in Zurich sold more than two dozen of his pictures. In 1941, the government of Canton Thurgau purchased its first Dietrich picture, and finally in 1942 the Kunsthaus Zürich put on a show that included over 70 of his pictures—at the time, the largest exhibition of his work.

At the same time, larger institutions were slow to purchase his paintings. Some exceptions were the Kunstverein Konstanz (1913) and the Kunstmuseum Winterthur (1926). Generally these purchases came about through individuals who admired Dietrich's work and often made private purchases as well: Franz Meyer and H.E. Mayenfisch (Kunstgesellschaft Zürich [Zurich Art Society]), Paul Fink and Hans Keller (Kunstverein Winterthur [Winterthur Art Association]), Heinrich Schmidt-Specht (Kunstverein Konstanz) and Heinrich Ammann (Kunstmuseum Thurgau).

WOODCUTTER, LABORER, FARMER—THE SWISS ROUSSEAU

Dietrich's pictures were particularly well-received in the media, which proved as easily seduced by the fairy-tale-like success story of the simple man from Thurgau as the other admirers of his work. Franz Roh writes in the "Neue Schweizer Rundschau" [New Swiss Review] in 1926 on "The Art of the Laborer, Farmer and Painter Adolf Dietrich. On the Problem of Amateur Art." And in 1927 Margot Riess published "The Painter and Woodcutter Adolf Dietrich."

Critics liked to compare Dietrich with Henri Rousseau. Karl Hoenn critically noted in his 1942 biography of Dietrich:

5. Karl Hoenn: Adolf Dietrich
(*Die Schweiz im deutschen
Geistesleben*, vol. 24), Frauenfeld /
Leipzig, 1942, p. 7.

"One frequently sees 'and woodcutter' appended to the designation 'painter' as if by way of apology, just as people persist in referring to Henri Rousseau as a 'douanier.'"[5] Dietrich's work finally reached a wider audience when it was reported on in the Swiss tabloids, which helped disseminate the myth of the simple genius.

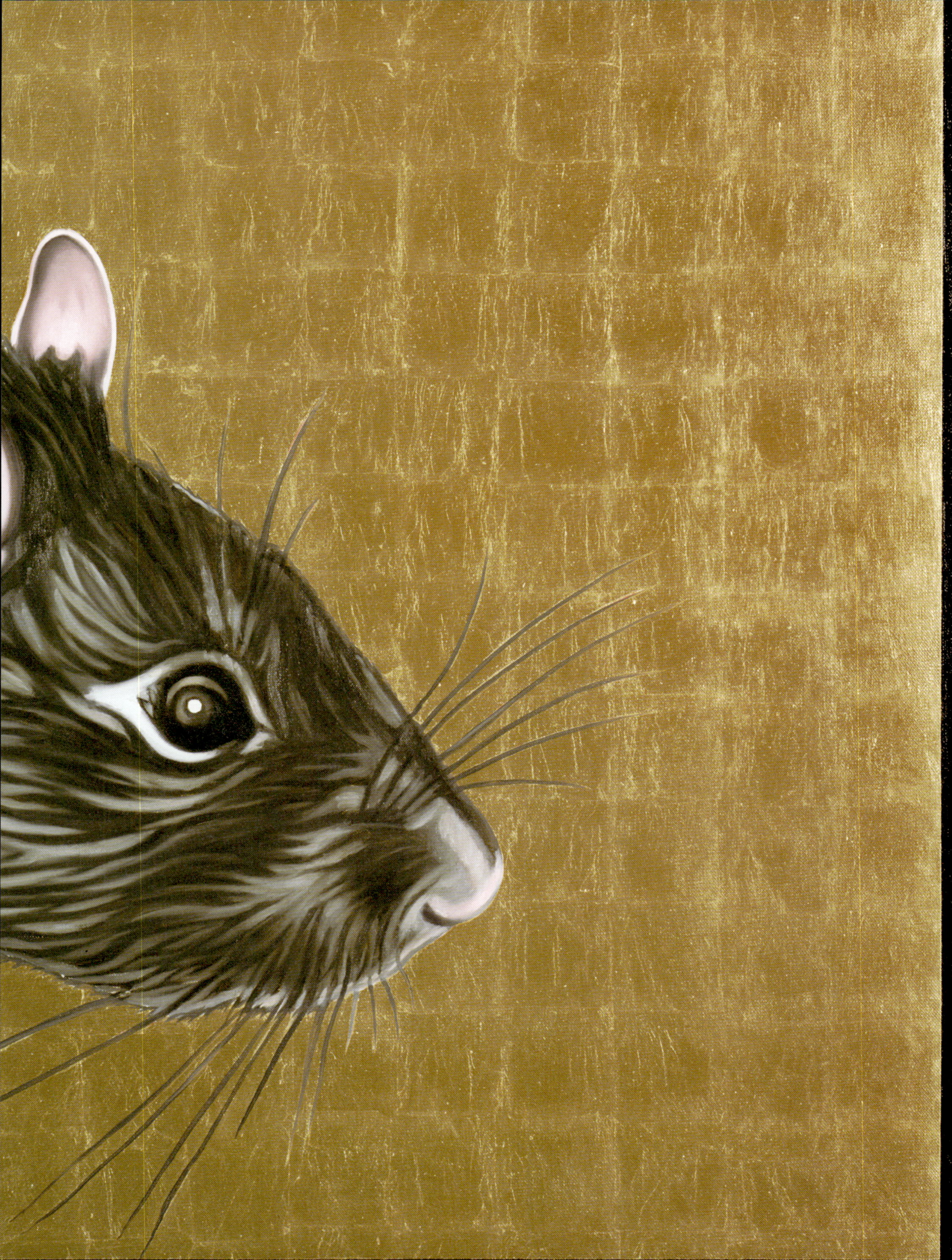

4/4:
Richard Phillips
Were You of Silver,
Were You of Gold?
2009
82 x 60 in. / 208.3 x 152.4 cm
Oil on linen
Courtesy of the artist and
Gagosian Gallery, New York

Since he was widely seen as an amateur artist, a naïve farmer/painter, Dietrich gained further popularity during the war—he was billed as a quintessentially "Swiss" artist, along with Albert Anker and Ferdinand Hodler, as part of widespread efforts to preserve a sense of Swiss cultural identity. His idyllic landscapes, genre paintings depicting (untouched) village life and animal pictures were popular in the media.

After Dietrich's breakthrough in Switzerland, the interest in his work remained constant. There was a continuous stream of visitors to his small house in Berlingen. So many people wanted to purchase his work that he wasn't able to keep up with the demand, and he started to copy and repaint some of his own pictures. When Adolf Dietrich died in 1957, he was a wealthy man. His taxable estate was valued at over 70,000 Swiss francs.

GENUINE, INNOCENT, ORIGINAL—THE AUTHENTIC ARTIST

Once Adolf Dietrich's artistic talent became known, the reports of third parties who had contact with or stories to tell about him met with unflagging interest, both among the general public and in the art world.

The qualities of childish innocence, naïveté and an original aesthetic approach were soon attributed to the Berlingen painter and stuck.
The concepts "real", "genuine" and "authentic" were frequently used in discussing his work and become important metaphors in its reception and evaluation. Such projections can be traced back to a desire to discover the ideal of a pure life, a desire for the "paradise on Earth" that one finds particularly well expressed in the work of a non-academic painter, an "outsider artist."

Behind this lies a basic need in our society for fairy tales and myths. Our longing for the genuine—for what is real—could, it seems, be found and grasped in exemplary form in the life and work of this Berlingen smallholder. The artist became the medium for an experience of authenticity.

THE "WRONG" RECEPTION AND ITS CAUSES

Various factors play a role in the one-sided reception of Dietrich's work—factors having to do both with social structures at the time and also with the nature of the art world and Dietrich's own idiosyncratic character. The art world has always been an elite system, and in Dietrich's time class distinctions were far more rigid than they are today. Dietrich's path to becoming a non-academic painter began with his parents' decision to keep their son home to help out despite his obvious talent, instead of letting him be educated as a lithographer, which would have paved the way for his training as an artist. Already in 1942 Karl Hoenn remarks: "It is not so much an artistic problem as a social one that individuals who are so eminently talented as artists are compelled to become customs agents [like Rousseau] and woodcutters and can pursue their inner calling only on the side."[6]

Dietrich's "discovery" by the art world during the interwar years was helped along by an already established interest on the part of the avant-garde in primitive, naïve and amateur art as well as that of the mentally ill and other categories used to describe

6. ibid., p. 7.

the work of those who were active as artists outside the academic art system. This can be seen among other things in the fact that Dietrich's own attempts in the early years of the century to be accepted into this system were met with failure, and he was dependent on help from individuals who were insiders in the system. That the protagonists of the German art market at the time considered Dietrich somewhat exotic, should not be held against them now. As art historian Ralf Schiebler puts it: "The 'timeliness' of truth pertains not only to truth itself but is a product of the historical circumstances in which one takes an interest in truth or not."[7]

Finally the letters from the artist's estate indicate that Dietrich himself had a hand in the developments taken by his career. Having grown up in deeply rural surroundings that were still marked by a barter system, he was overwhelmed by the wave of success and the new forms of social interaction it required of him. Modern, urban modes of interaction now stood in sharp contrast to a rurally organized mode of living.

He himself had a mixed reaction to the ever-increasing demands of his customers. He would promise pictures and then sell them to someone else altogether, sidestepping all responsibility by having the customers who'd reserved the same picture fight things out among themselves, and finding support from individuals who enjoyed acting as protectors to this supposedly childish and naïve farmer—supporters who then would accuse one another of exploiting him.

RIGHT AND WRONG IMAGES

Coupled with the desire for authenticity is the wish to experience the definitive image of the artist—in other words the right one. But isn't all the information about a person that we collect, cull, interpret and pass along a projection and therefore, in the end, a sort of myth-making? Even the "scholar most committed to thorough research," writes Ralph Schiebler, will "because of the haphazardness of the information he is able to access and the limitations of his own horizons have to create a new myth once the old ones are demolished."[8] What we know today about the life and work of an artist is comprised of the most various, subjectively experienced images promulgated through the media, making it a playground for projections.

But there's also something positive about this one-sided reception. A person who—for whatever reasons—occupies himself with Adolf Dietrich's pictures will experience the marvelous feeling of being able to discover Dietrich's art and even the artist himself as if for the first time. For despite the many publications and all the stories that have been told about Dietrich, his autonomous oeuvre, unique in the history of art, can never be entirely fathomed and thus remains enigmatic—an impression paradoxically linked to the feeling of uniqueness and authenticity that surrounds his work. This makes him—very much in the sense of Baudrillard's "mirroring"—an artist whose work reflects the viewer back at himself.

7. Ralph Schiebler: "Mythen– und Dogmenbildung in Kunst und Kunstgeschichtsschreibung. Ein Dialog mit Rainer Walther," in: *Genie und Wahnsinn und andere Artikel zwischen Kunst und Wissenschaft,* Stuttgart / Zürich 1984, p. 172.

8. ibid., p. 173.

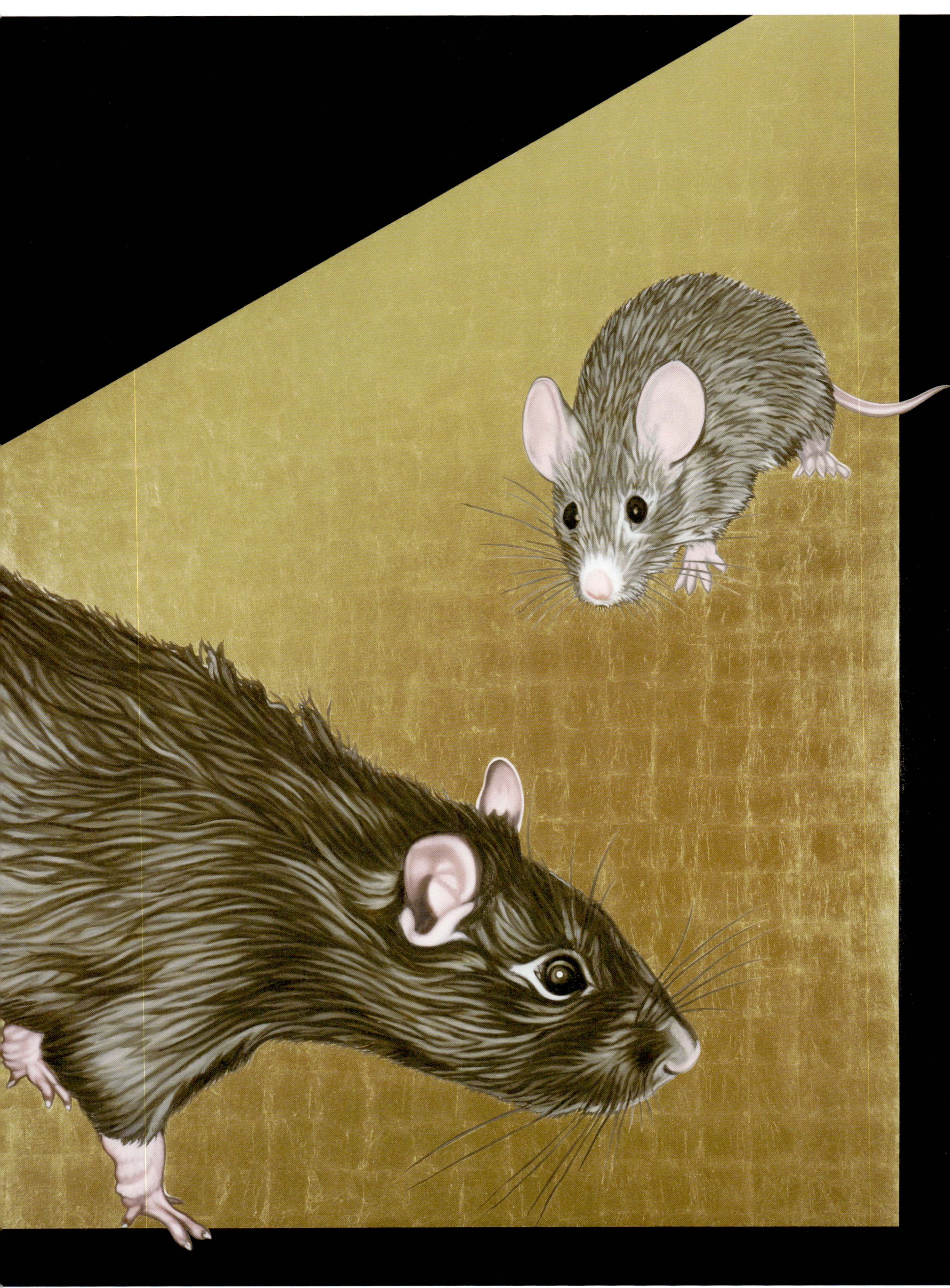

1/4–4/4. and Left–right:
Richard Phillips
<u>Were You of Silver,</u>
<u>Were You of Gold?</u>
2009
82 x 60 in. / 208.3 x 152.4 cm
Oil on linen
Courtesy of the artist and
Gagosian Gallery, New York

Adolf Dietrich
<u>Mausefalle mit 22 Mäusen</u>
1948
11 x 12 in. / 28 x 30.5 cm
Oil on cardboard
Kunstmuseum des Kantons Thurgau,
Ittinger Museum

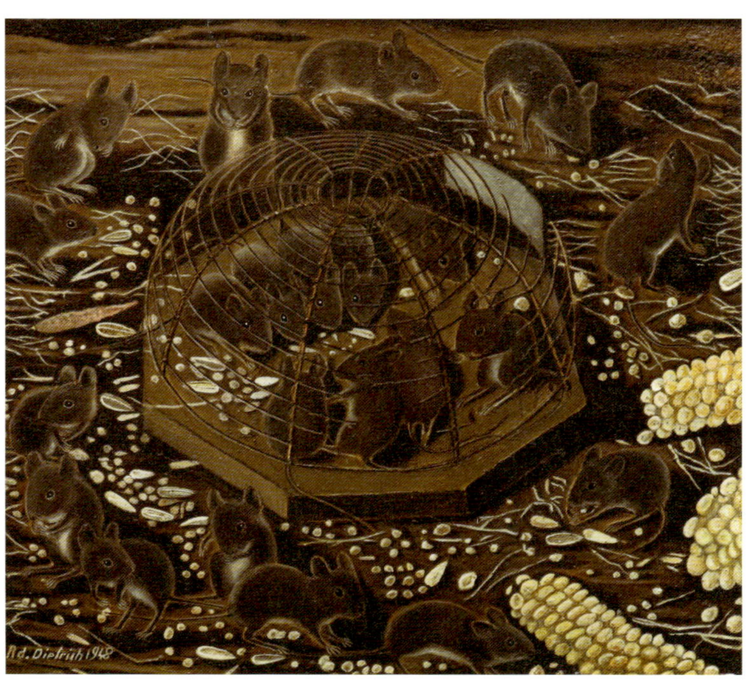

Adolf Dietrich
Gelbroter Abendhimmel
1925
15.2 x 24 in. / 38.5 x 61 cm
Oil on cardboard
Kunstmuseum des Kantons Thurgau,
Ittinger Museum

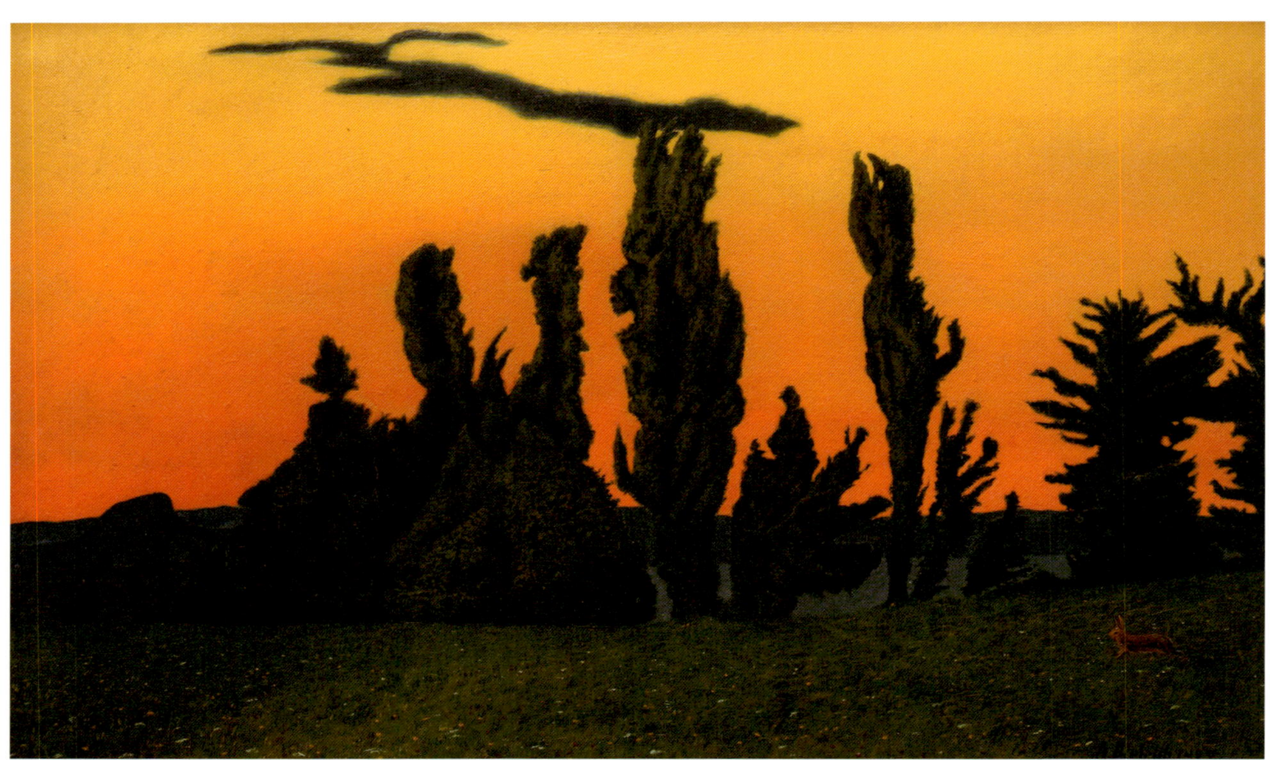

Adolf Dietrich
Hermelin und tote Möwe in
Mondscheinlandschaft
1908
18.9 x 13.6 in. / 48 x 34.5 cm
Oil on canvas
Kunstmuseum des Kantons Thurgau,
Ittinger Museum

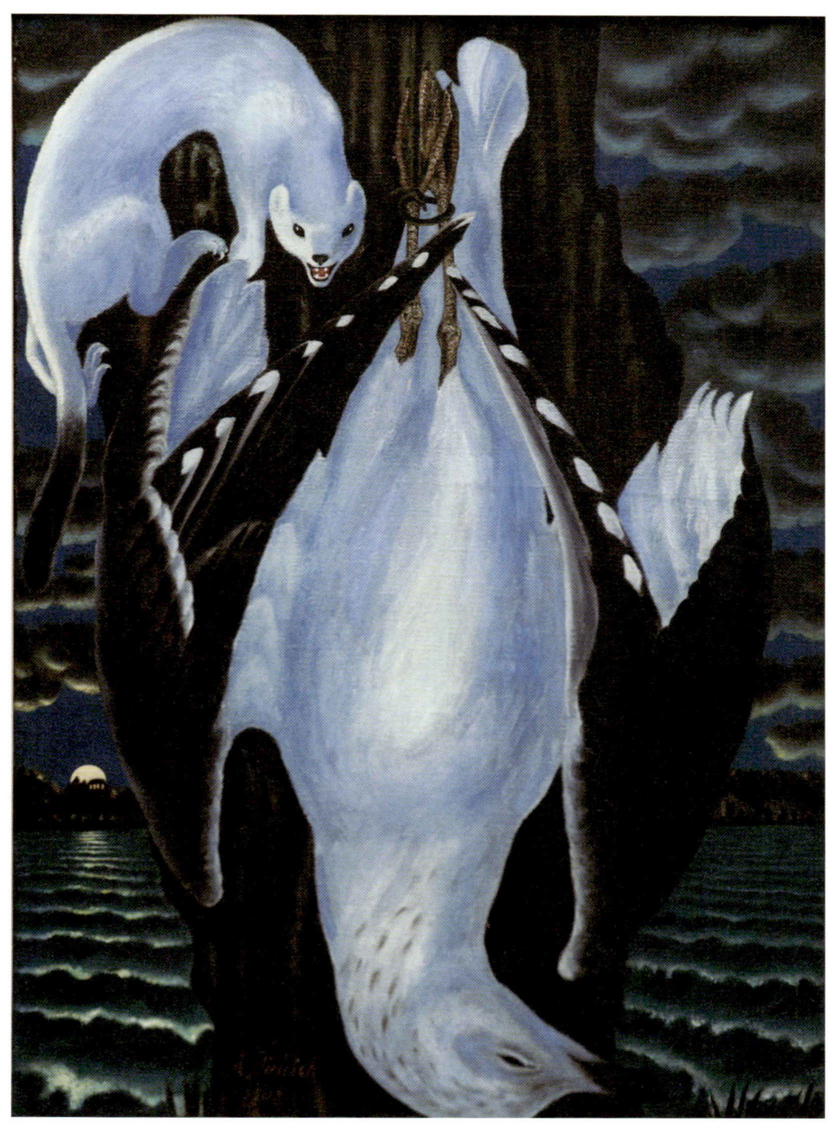

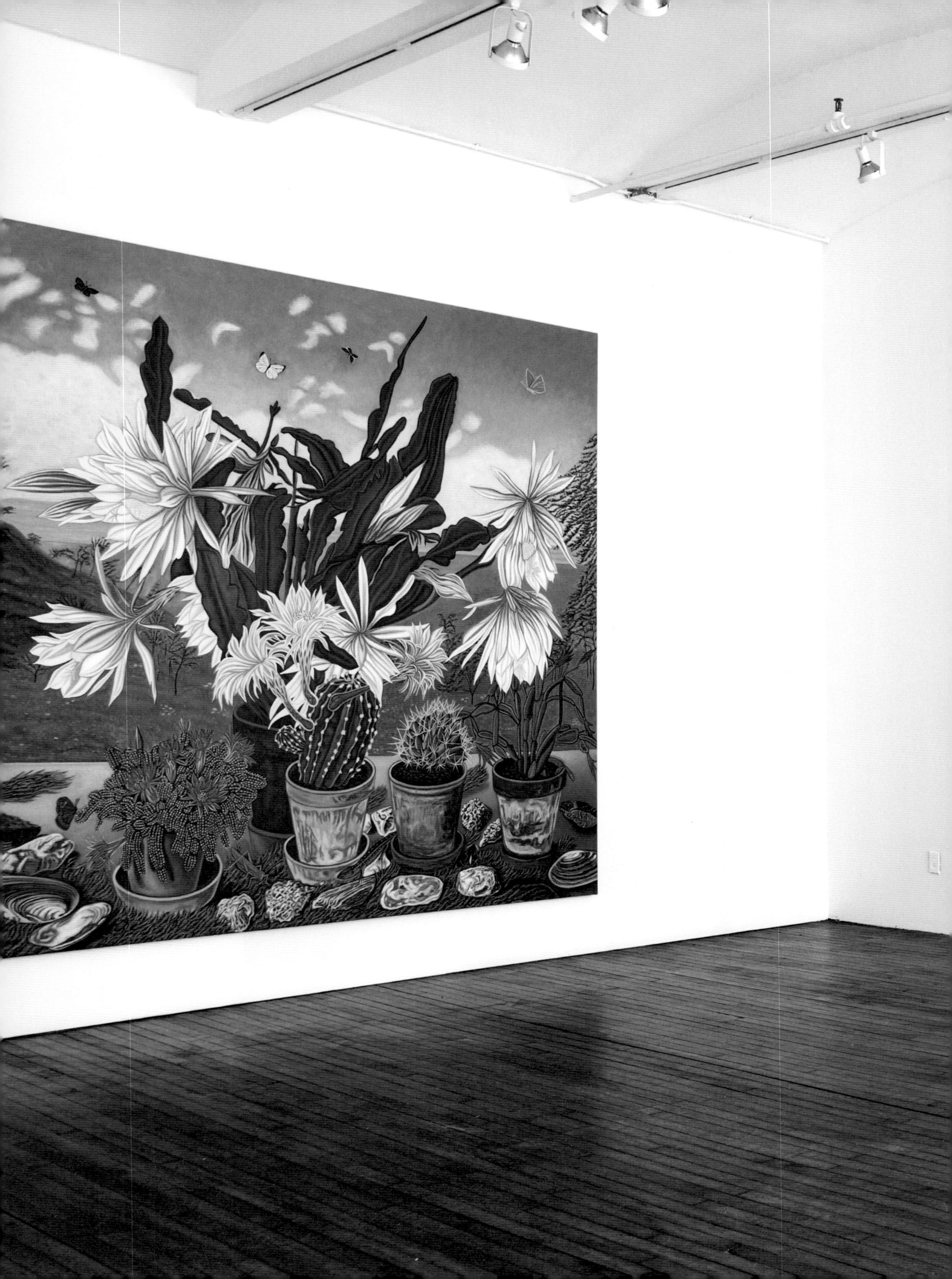

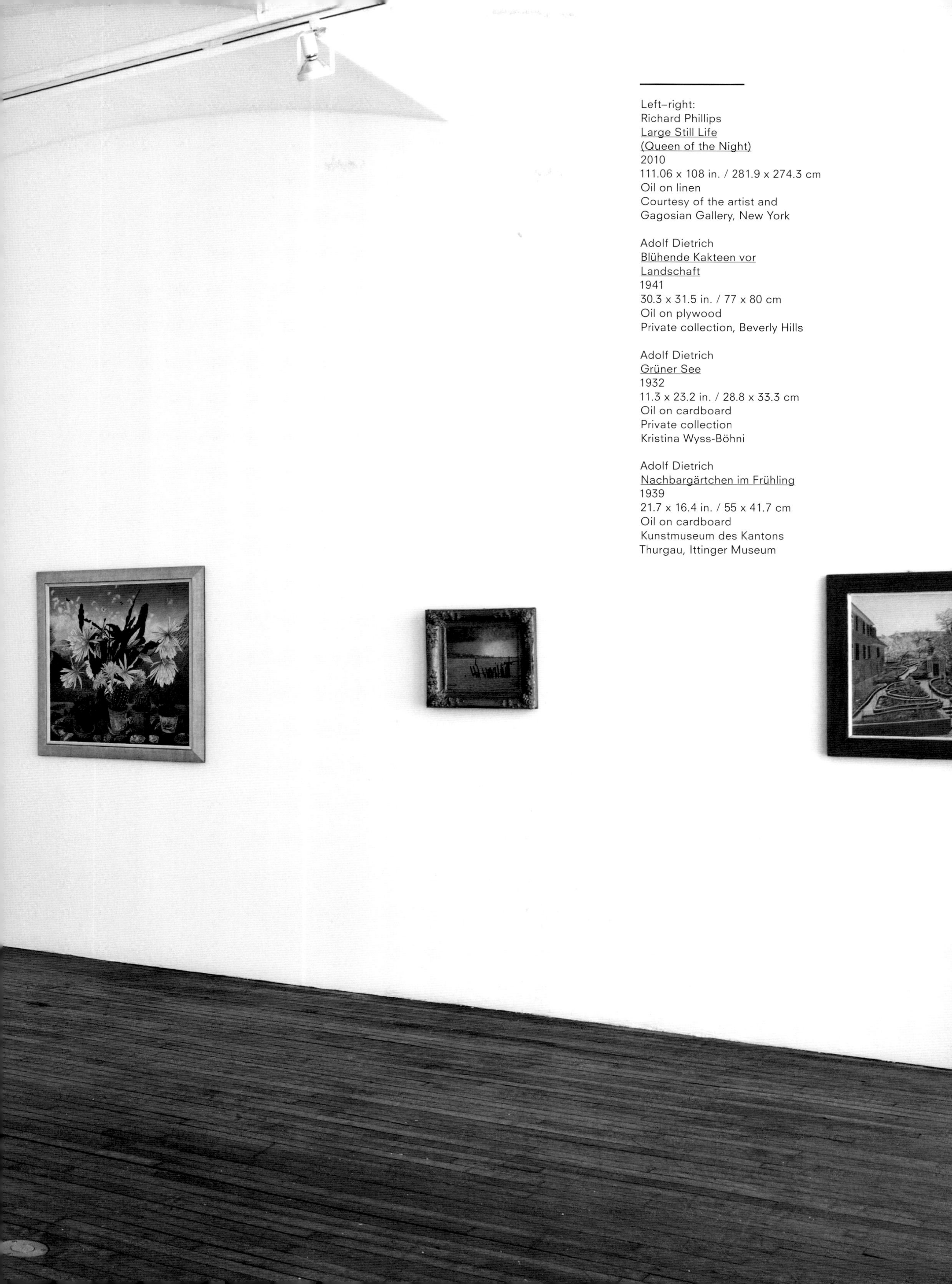

Left–right:
Richard Phillips
Large Still Life
(Queen of the Night)
2010
111.06 x 108 in. / 281.9 x 274.3 cm
Oil on linen
Courtesy of the artist and
Gagosian Gallery, New York

Adolf Dietrich
Blühende Kakteen vor
Landschaft
1941
30.3 x 31.5 in. / 77 x 80 cm
Oil on plywood
Private collection, Beverly Hills

Adolf Dietrich
Grüner See
1932
11.3 x 23.2 in. / 28.8 x 33.3 cm
Oil on cardboard
Private collection
Kristina Wyss-Böhni

Adolf Dietrich
Nachbargärtchen im Frühling
1939
21.7 x 16.4 in. / 55 x 41.7 cm
Oil on cardboard
Kunstmuseum des Kantons
Thurgau, Ittinger Museum

Left–right:
Adolf Dietrich
<u>Kaninchen und Aquarium</u>
1939
11.6 x 9.1 in. / 29.5 x 23 cm
Oil on cardboard
Private collection

Adolf Dietrich
<u>Pfeffervogel</u>
1927
18.1 x 15 in. / 46 x 38 cm
Oil on cardboard
Städtische Museen Konstanz

Adolf Dietrich
<u>Eichhörnchenbild / Zwei
Eichhörnchen
in Landschaft</u>
1939
24.4 x 17.1 in. / 62 x 43.5 cm
Oil on cardboard
Private collection

Richard Phillips
<u>Similar to Squirrels (after A. Dietrich)</u>
2003
102.5 x 78 in. / 260.4 x 198.1 cm
Oil on linen
Hall Collection

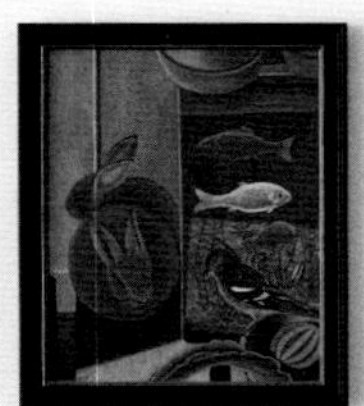

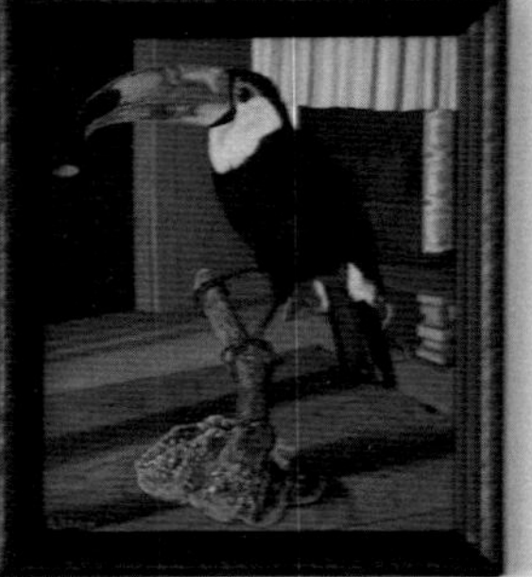

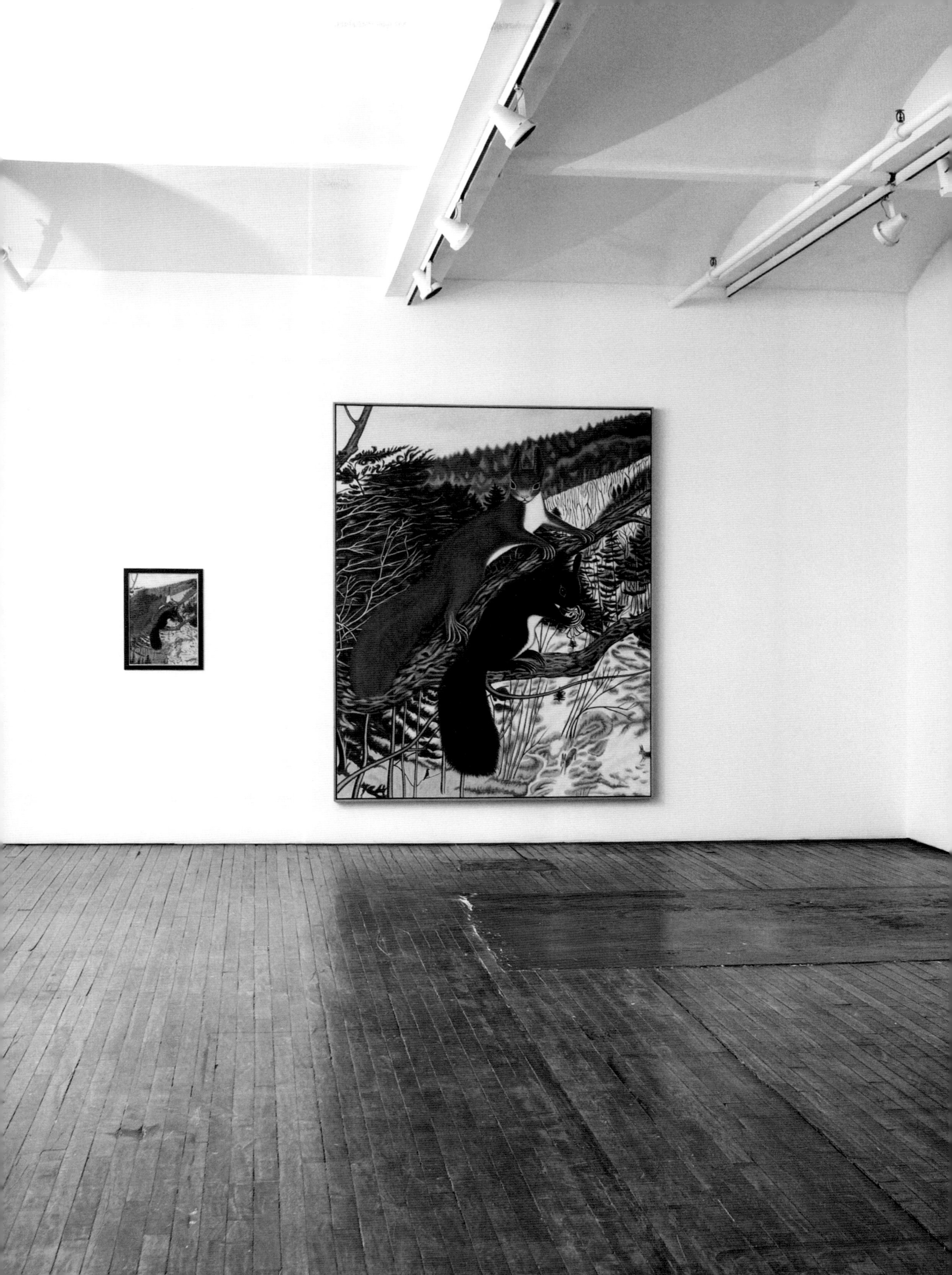

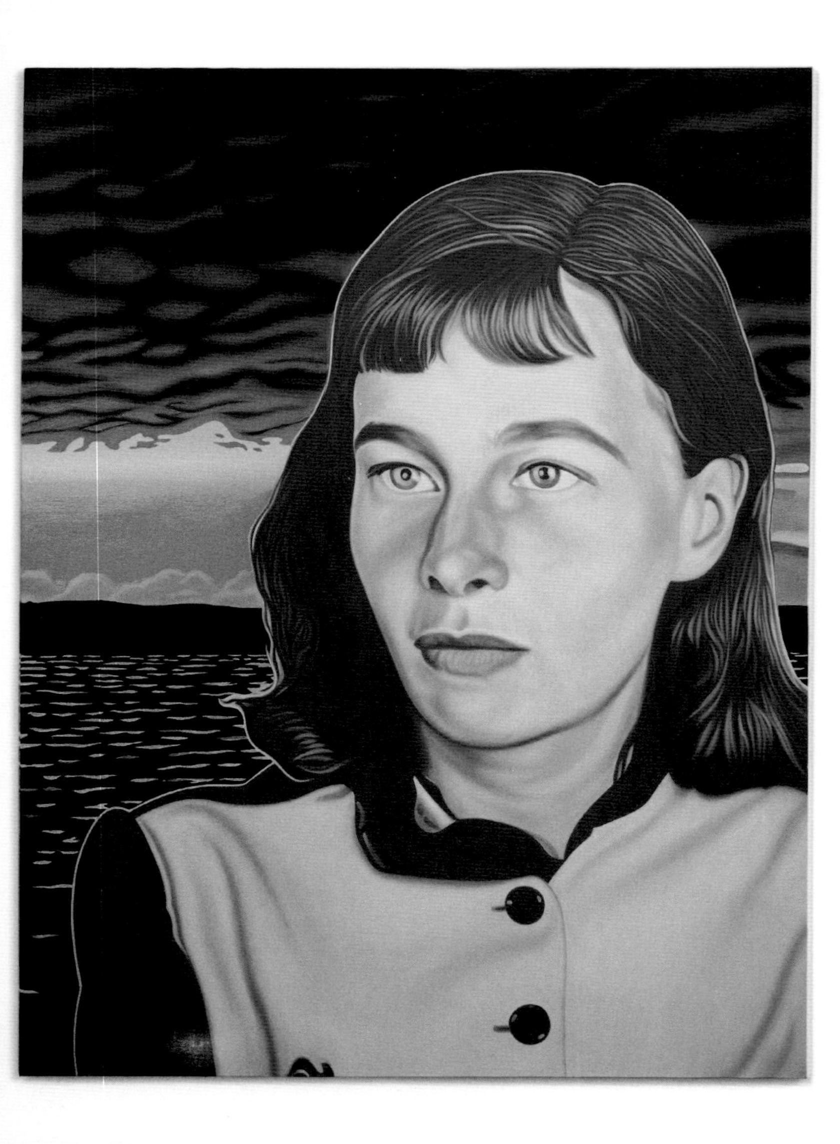
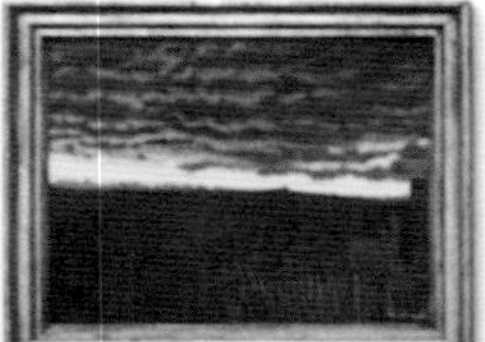
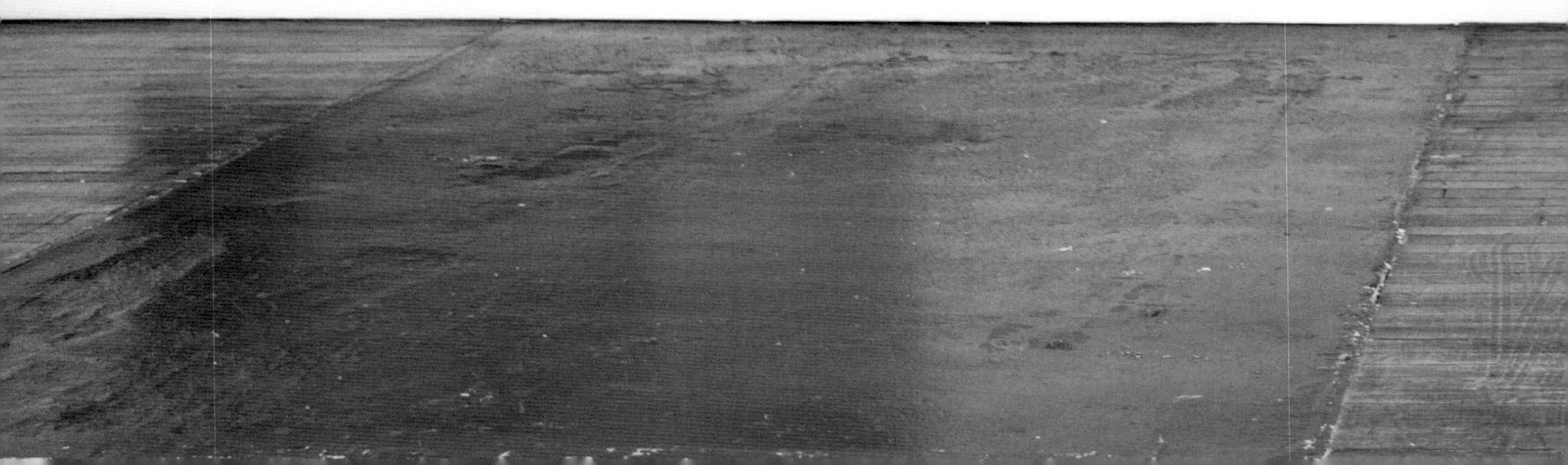

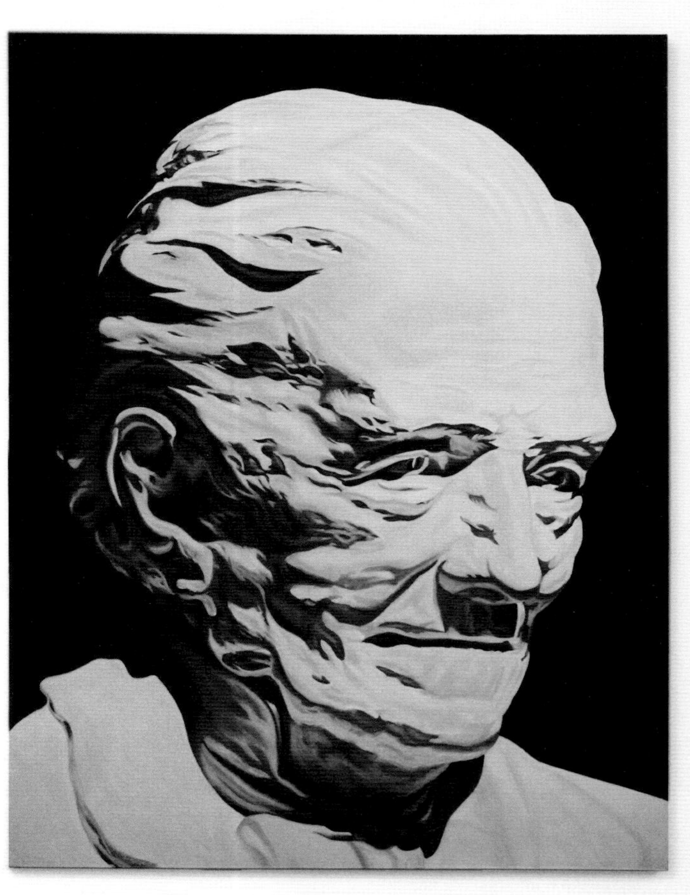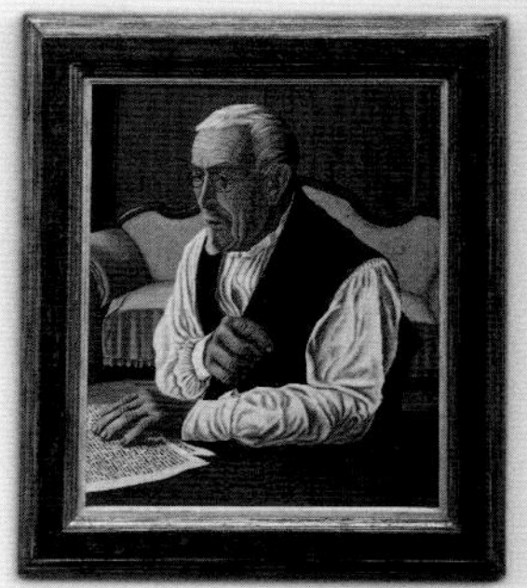

Left–right:
Richard Phillips
Libertas
2010
102 x 79.3 in. / 229.1 x 201.4 cm
Oil on linen
Courtesy of the artist and Gagosian
Gallery, New York

Adolf Dietrich
Abend am Untersee
1918
15 x 19.3 in. / 38.1 x 49 cm
Oil on plywood
Neue Nationalgalerie, Berlin

Richard Phillips
Old Granddad
2001
84 x 65.5 in. / 213.4 x 166.6 cm
Oil on canvas
Private collection

Adolf Dietrich
Vater, die Zeitung lesend
1913
24 x 20.1 in. / 61 x 51 cm
Oil on canvas
Kunstmuseum des Kantons Thurgau,
Ittinger Museum

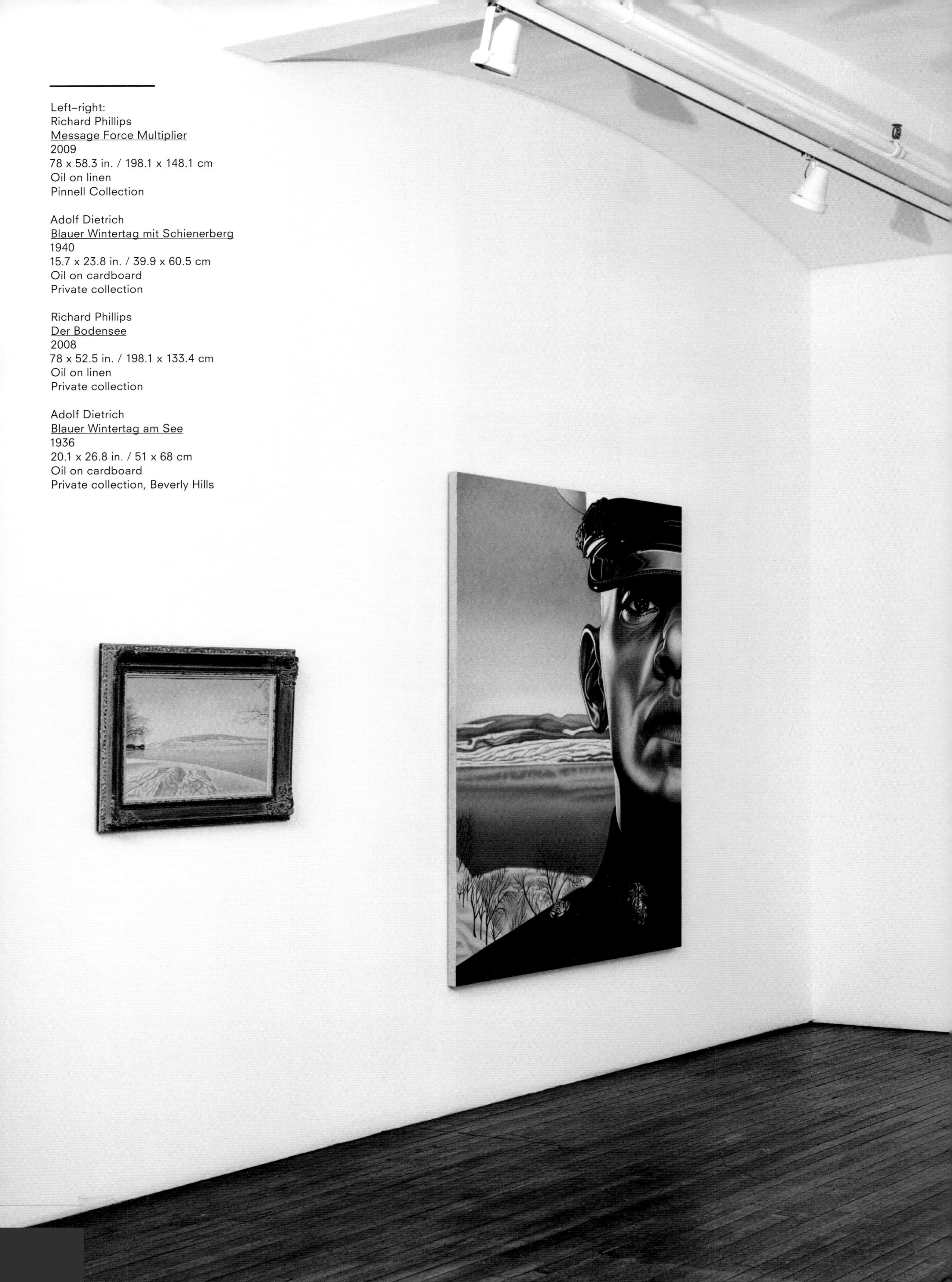

Left–right:
Richard Phillips
Message Force Multiplier
2009
78 x 58.3 in. / 198.1 x 148.1 cm
Oil on linen
Pinnell Collection

Adolf Dietrich
Blauer Wintertag mit Schienerberg
1940
15.7 x 23.8 in. / 39.9 x 60.5 cm
Oil on cardboard
Private collection

Richard Phillips
Der Bodensee
2008
78 x 52.5 in. / 198.1 x 133.4 cm
Oil on linen
Private collection

Adolf Dietrich
Blauer Wintertag am See
1936
20.1 x 26.8 in. / 51 x 68 cm
Oil on cardboard
Private collection, Beverly Hills

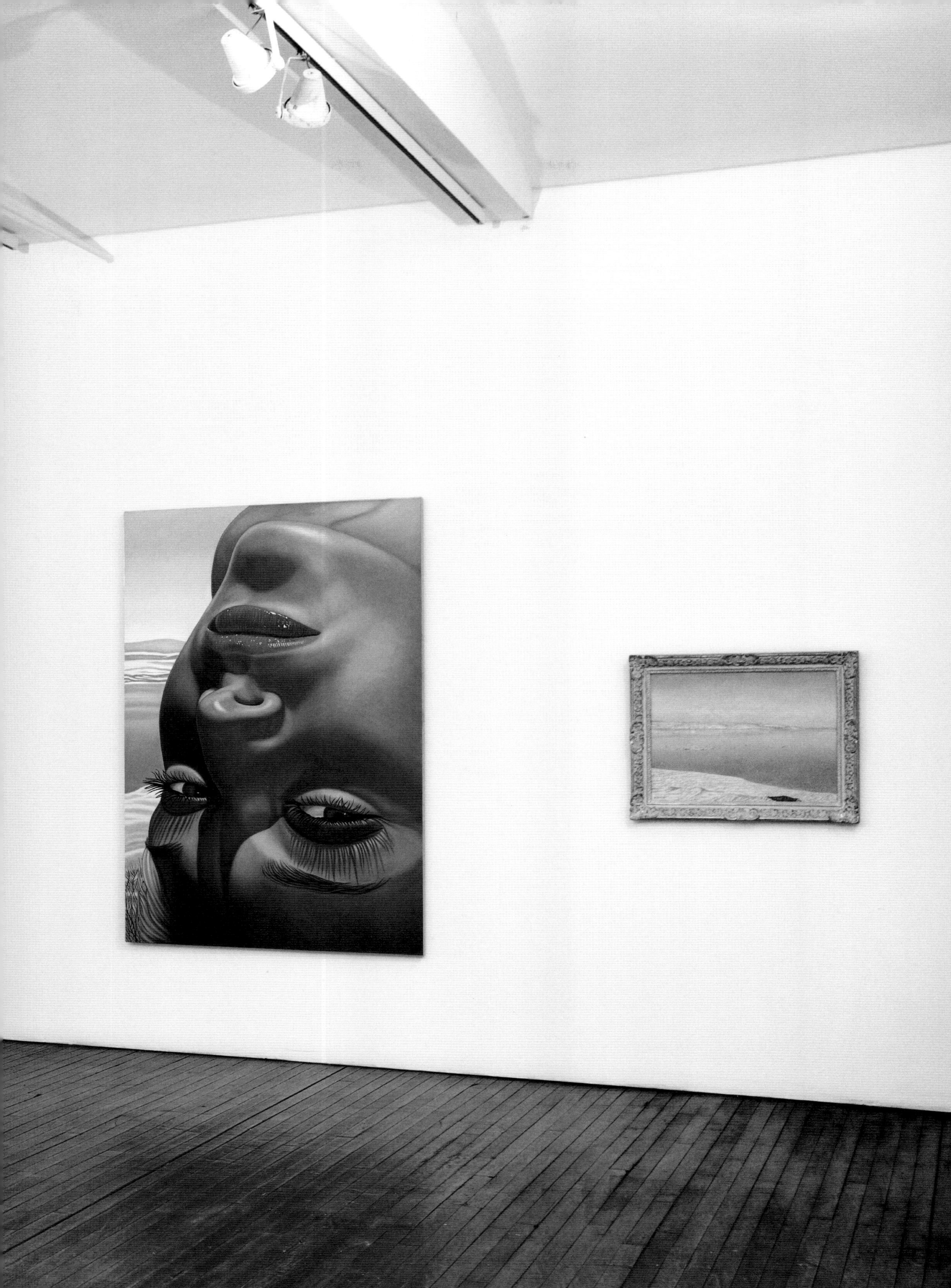

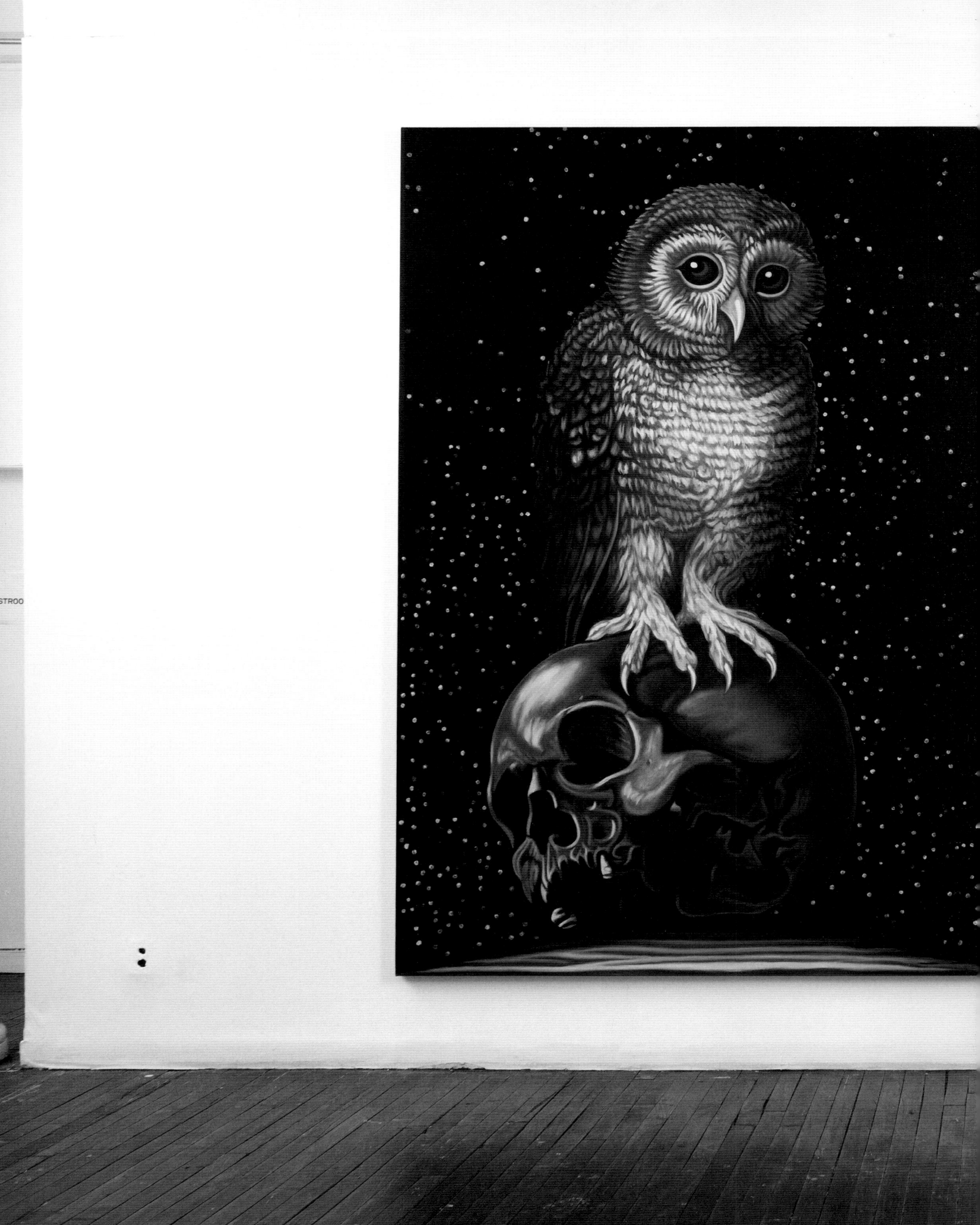
STROO

Left–right:
Richard Phillips
<u>Vanitas</u>
2007
108 x 74 in. / 274.3 x 188 cm
Oil on linen
Private collection

Adolf Dietrich
<u>Waldkäuze im Tobel</u>
1929
33.1 x 23.2 in. / 84 x 59 cm
Oil on cardboard
Private collection

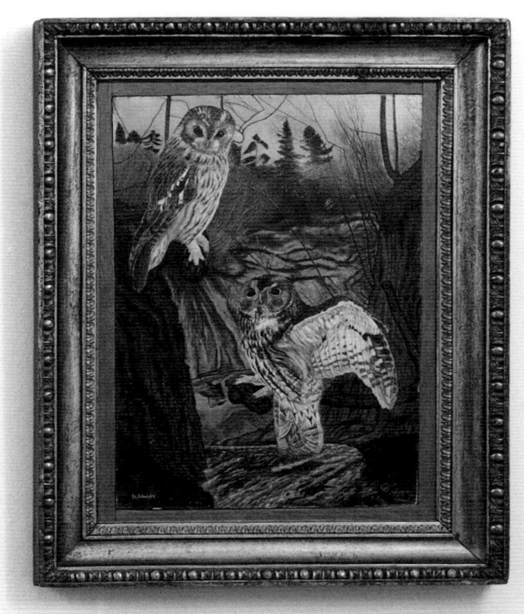

Left–right:
Adolf Dietrich
<u>Zwei Angorakätzchen</u>
1925
14.4 x 13.6 in. / 36.5 x 34.5 cm
Oil on cardboard
Private collection

Richard Phillips
<u>Mouser</u>
1997
16 x 20 in. / 40.6 x 50.8 cm
Oil on linen
Private collection

Adolf Dietrich
<u>Zaine mit jungen Kätzchen</u>
1934
16.5 x 19.9 in. / 42 x 50.5 cm
Oil on plywood
Private collection

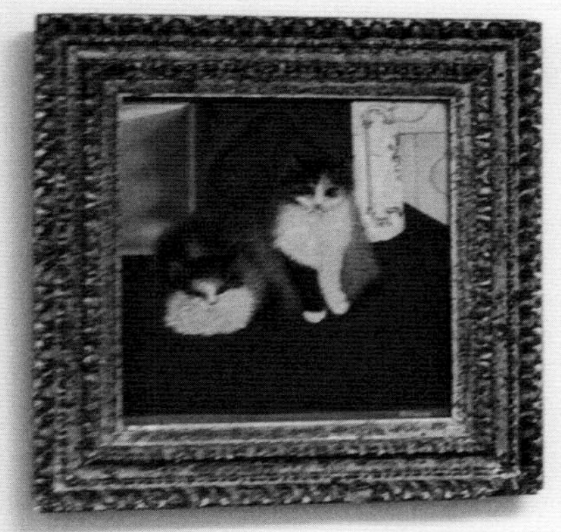

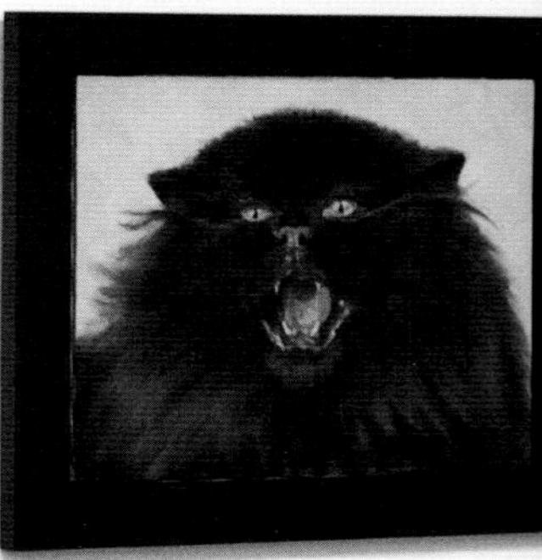

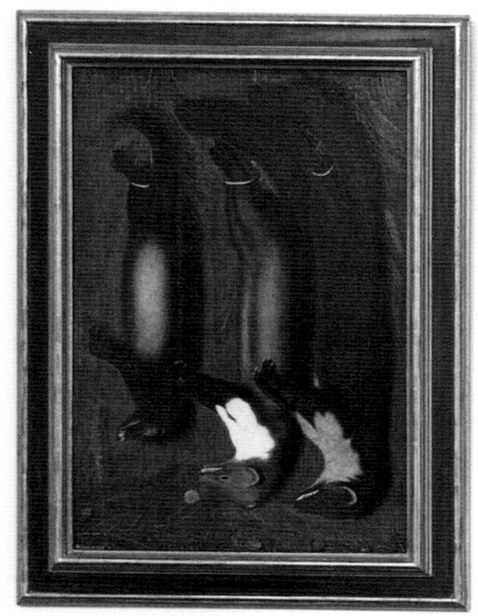

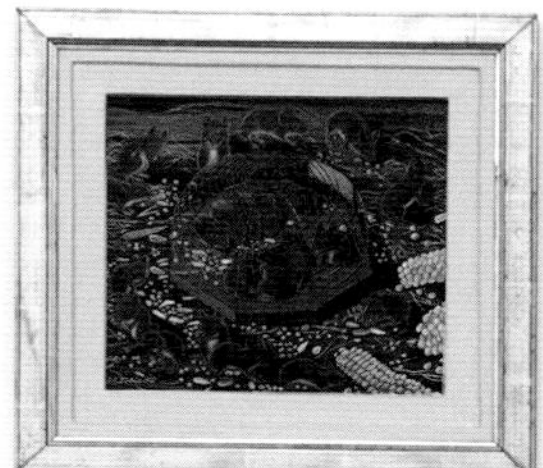

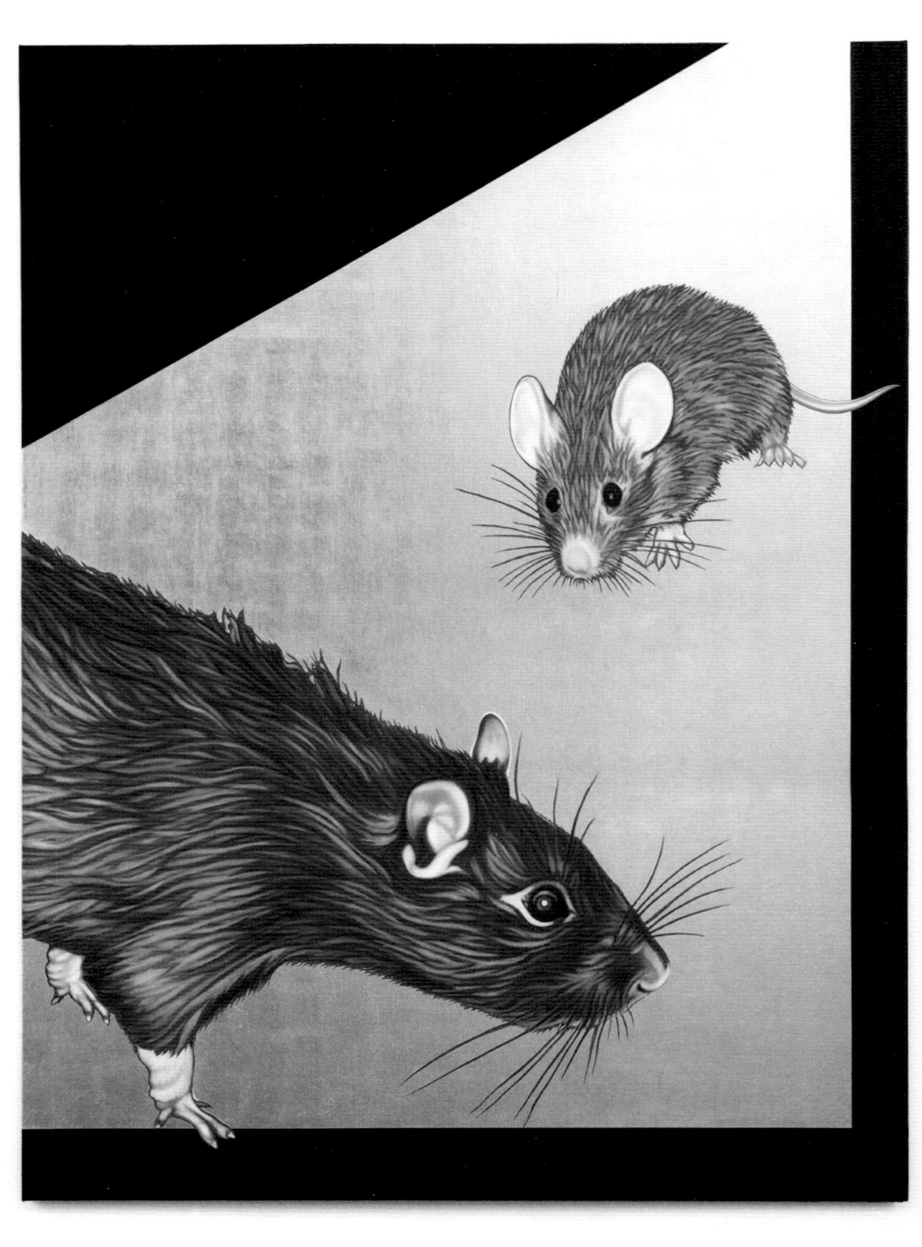

Left–right:
Adolf Dietrich
<u>Gelbroter Abendhimmel</u>
1925
15.2 x 24 in. / 38.5 x 61 cm
Oil on plywood
Kunstmuseum des Kantons Thurgau, Ittinger
Museum

Adolf Dietrich
<u>Hermelin und tote Möwe in
Mondscheinlandschaft</u>
1908
18.9 x 13.6 in. / 48 x 34.5 cm
Oil on canvas
Kunstmuseum des Kantons Thurgau, Ittinger
Museum

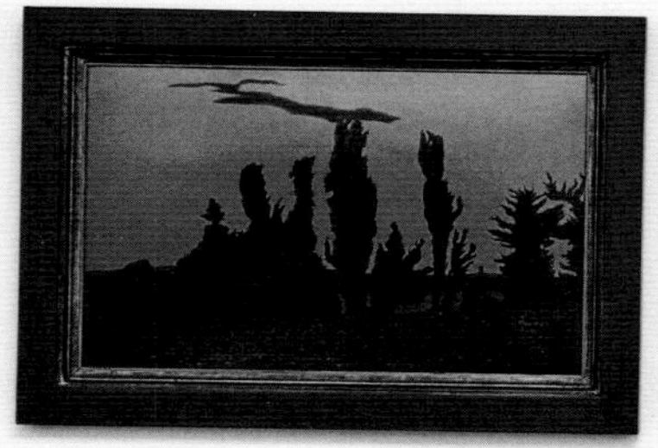

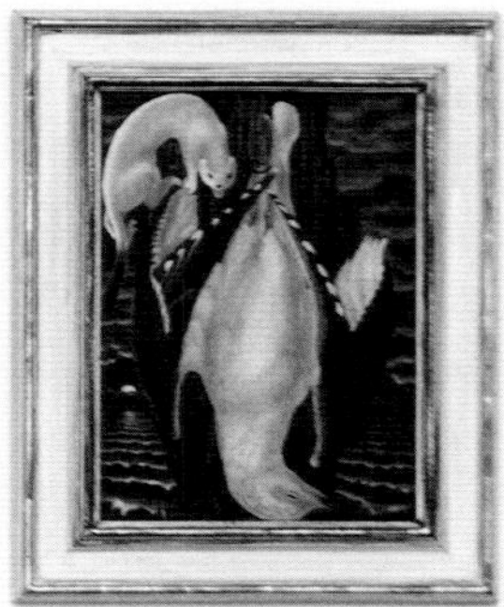